EXPERT
OWNERSHIP

Launching Faith-Filled Entrepreneurs into Greater Freedom and Success

DAVID AND JASON BENHAM

Nationally Acclaimed Entrepreneurs, Bestselling Authors, SeeYaPreneurs

Learn more about the brothers at BenhamBrothers.com.
Learn more about Expert Ownership at ExpertOwnership.com.

Published in Charlotte, North Carolina, by Benham Media. Published in
association with the literary agency of WTA Services, LLC, Franklin, TN.

Unless otherwise indicated, Scripture quotations are taken from the Holy Bible,
New International Version* and New American Standard Bible*…

…New International Version*, NIV*. © 1973, 1978, 1984, 2011 by Biblica,
Inc.* Used by permission of Zondervan. All rights reserved worldwide.

…New American Standard Bible*, NASB*. ©
1960, 1962, 1963, 1968, 1971, 1972, 1973, 1975, 1977, 1995
by The Lockman Foundation. Used by permission.

Editors – Bonita Jewel, Karla Dial.

Cover and interior design by Diegeo De La Rosa.
Cover photograph by Gregory Woodman

ISBN: 978-1-7368070-8-8
e-book ISBN: 978-1-7368070-1-9
audio book ISBN: 978-1-7368070-2-6

Library of Congress Control Number: 2021904574
Printed in the United States of America

Bulk purchases available. Contact through BenhamBrothers.com.

ENDORSEMENTS

WHAT LEADERS ARE SAYING:

"David and Jason show you how to achieve incredible success by making God and family the cornerstones of your life."

Dave Ramsey, President, Ramsey Solutions

"David and Jason's business success is similar to our own - God's grace and a lot of grit. I love these guys!"

Curt Richardson, Founder, Otter Box

"The Benham boys have got it down straight!"

Phil Robertson, Duck Dynasty & Duck Commander

"The Benhams will challenge your integrity and self-discipline, then leave you fired up to live your faith!"

Alex Kendrick, Movie Producer,
NY Times #1 Best-Selling Author

"The Benham's always remind me that our business is our ministry, and they've modeled many key principles we apply like delivering value and being a fountain not a drain!"

Dave Alpern, President, Joe Gibbs Racing

WHAT ENTREPRENEURS ARE SAYING:

"David and Jason have the God-given ability to speak directly into specific problems or roadblocks, as well as the foresight to point out things you might not be thinking about. And they truly love people - combine that with their innate business sense and you're left with a lasting impact!"

Landon & Kat Eckles, Founders Clean Juice

"I brought my entire team of managers to their office, and the brothers poured into them with Bible-based kingdom principles that revolutionized the way my team saw their work. I've enjoyed watching them work with newfound purpose and passion!"

Andy Osbolt, Zaxby's

"In just one hour working through the Benham's 4S model, my paradigm for business completely changed. I'm finally going to be able to become the absentee owner I've always wanted to be!"

Brian Echevarria, Founder C3 Coffee

"I bet even Ray Kroc could take some pointers on workflow management from the Benham boys! Impressive stuff - anyone who applies the content should easily see a 10x return on their investment."

Garrett White, Co-Owner 1st Place Turf

"Insights from David and Jason have taken my business from $250k in revenue to over $1mm. But revenue is just the tip of the iceberg, they have provided the direction and guidance that has allowed me to quickly identify and resolve any potential road-blocks within our growth cycle."

Steve Pinkerton, Owner Crossfit Vitality

"Over eight years of business growth, I craved mentorship and advice. I found it with Benham Brothers' Expert Ownership! Even while taking the class I was able to immediately put lessons learned into action -- which helped me make hiring decisions and organize my business in a way to truly scale."

Brian Jackson, Owner, Mighty Missouri Coffee Co

WHAT CHRISTIAN LEADERS ARE SAYING:

"The Benham's have decided both privately and publicly to take their stand as Christians. Not willing to hang out in the closet of spiritual complacency, they have positioned themselves as beacons of light in the midst of cultural compromise and spiritual mediocrity."

Dr. Tony Evans, Pastor & Best-Selling Author

"In all my years of ministry, rarely have I seen a more desperate time when we need courageous Christians to rise up. We need modern- day Daniels who will take a stand and refuse to compromise their faith. These two men live out this message, and I am proud to call them friends."

Dr. Charles Stanley, Sr Pastor First Baptist Atlanta

"David and Jason's story will move you with compassion and challenge you with resolve to stand on the firm foundation of God's Word—whatever the cost!"

Franklin Graham, President, Billy Graham
Evangelistic Association

"Jason and David Benham are the enemy's worst nightmare. Their steadfast faith, unwavering commitment to God and unashamed zeal for His Word are a serious threat to the kingdom of darkness in our culture."

Priscilla Shirer, Bible Teacher & NYT Best-Selling Author

"Full of wit and wisdom the Benham's teach and encourage us to live a fully integrated life pleasing to God regardless of the cost. The way they uncover the identity of workplace Christians as ministers on mission is life changing."

Ken Eldred, President, Ziklag Group

ACKNOWLEDGMENTS

No one builds a business on their own. Though you may go faster alone, you'll only go further together. There are those God places along your path to take you further than you imagined. Here are a few we'd like to thank:

Allen Craven, our first real estate boss – thank you for giving us a chance, showing us the ropes, and then blessing us to go out and do our own thing. Few business owners would have done that.

Tim Harrell, our college roommate and business partner – thank you for being our best pal, for analyzing every business deal we've ever done, and for sticking with us whenever we jumped in. Without you, we'd still be mowing lawns today.

David Traugott, our good buddy who encouraged us to impact more people by going digital – thank you for walking with us as we parsed through mountains of content from our business journey. And thank you for showing us how to listen to the Holy Spirit's whisper. You helped us hear God in ways we'd never heard before.

Our Expert Ownership core team: Larry Hubatka, Trey Sheneman, Sarah Bush, and Brian Dixon – We've heard it said that the best business owners surround themselves with people smarter and better than they are, which is certainly our case with you all. We love you guys and thank you sincerely. Glad we're on this journey together.

Jeremy Boering & Caleb Robinson: You men have built Daily Wire into a media empire. What you've accomplished in such a short amount of time, from proof of concept to global scale, is nothing short of miraculous. You are true expert owners. And you inspired us to think big ... no, really big! Thank you. This book doesn't happen without both of you.

To all our former employees and franchisees – thank you for being patient with us. We had no clue what we were doing, but you gave us grace and space to figure it out. Together with you, we built something special. Thank you!

TABLE OF CONTENTS

INTRODUCTION

Our business careers started shortly after we got out of professional baseball. Neither of us had any formal training whatsoever—no classes, no books, nothing. We were history majors at Liberty University, which was basically a degree to work toward while waiting for the Major League draft. But we were armed with the principles and stories of the Bible, passed down to us by our pastor dad. He taught us to love the Bible and apply it to every area of our lives. The more we applied its principles to our work, the more we realized Scripture was a manual for business development.

Upon launching into the business world, we learned that God's Word not only leads people to experience *spiritual* freedom but freedom *in every area of life*, including *the financial arena*. And the more we focused on building our business on Scripture, the more we discovered the Bible contains firsthand secrets to success in the marketplace. In short, it taught us to be what we now call "Expert Owners."

With the Bible as our guide, we were able to develop a family of businesses that grew to multiple companies—both for-profit and nonprofit—across the nation and in other parts of the world. And by the ripe old age of thirty-three, the two of us had transitioned from entrepreneurs to SeeYaPreneurs … as in, "See ya! We're out!"

We had achieved financial freedom and no longer needed a business to sustain us at all. We could keep working if we *wanted*, but we didn't *need* to keep trudging away. By God's grace, we had transcended the rat race,[1] which is the ultimate financial goal of Expert Owners.

Once you reach the level of SeeYaPreneur, all you really need to do is focus on impact for the rest of your life. You can start another business, build a nonprofit, serve in some other form of ministry—whatever you want ... because you're a SeeYaPreneur.

Here's the best part: If *we* became SeeYaPreneurs, then *you* can do it, too. We're not the brightest bulbs in the box. But as long as finding this level of business success lines up with God's will for your life, nothing can hold you back from achieving it. If you combine a disciplined work ethic with a commitment to do business God's way, then just buckle up and watch what happens.

But please hear us: None of this will amount to anything if you gain it all and miss the mark—*the divine purpose God has for your life and the people He's entrusted to your care.*

We know how to build a business. We know how to make money. But we also know those things don't mean squat if you have to forfeit key relationships to make it happen.

It means nothing to land a million-dollar deal if your daughter won't talk to you. What does it matter if your company is worth half a billion when divorce papers are sitting on your desk? Who the heck cares that you own a private jet if you're walking away from God's will?

This was the beauty of building our business on the principles of the Bible; it continually reminded us of what true success was. It wasn't defined in terms of money or accolades or opening new locations. It was defined by thriving relationships—with God and people—and impacting those

---

[1] Robert Kyosaki, *Rich Dad, Poor Dad* (Warner Books, 2000).

relationships for His glory.

You see, the question is not, "How good is my business?" or "How much money do I make?" The question is, "How deep are my relationships and how can I use my business to bless the other people in them?"

The Bible is a book about relationships—between God and the people He created. He blesses us so we can bless others. And if you can master relationships, you can excel in business (provided you implement some of the practical things we discuss in this book).

Every new business we open gets the same message:

- Our core is relationships.
- Our foundation is the Bible.
- Our goal is LIFE.

We want to breathe life into communities across the globe through the avenue of business based upon biblical principles.

But here's a crucial fact: The Bible isn't just a guide for relationships at home and a manual for success at work; it's also a weapon for battle against the devil and his schemes. When you apply God's Word to your life, you'll find that not only does success chase you down ... so does trouble.

We discovered this in the spring of 2014 after we signed a deal with HGTV to do a reality show on our business. Shortly after we started filming, and as commercials on our show began to run, liberal activists demanded the network pull the plug. They didn't like how vocal we were about faith in God and His design for marriage and the unborn.

Long before HGTV came our way, we felt God wanted us to use our voices to speak out about the moral evil taking place in our culture. Specifically, we knew God wanted us to *do something* about the plight of the unborn and *say something* about the redefinition of marriage. Plenty of other businesses pumped millions of dollars into Planned Parenthood and voiced their support for the redefinition of marriage, so we decided to do the same—just on the other side (the unpopular side).

We admit that doing this was much easier *before* we had experienced any success. Yet with a thriving national brand and a reality show on the line, the ballgame changed. If we spoke up, we'd better make sure to buckle up—because it could cost us something.

And cost us, it did. The pressure from the activist groups was so extreme that a few months before our show was set to air, HGTV fired us.

We found ourselves living out a great dichotomy: Applying the truths of the Bible to our *work* brought us promotion, but applying them to our *walk* brought us persecution. The same principles that got us hired got us fired.

You may have heard that part of our story before. We shared it in our first book, *Whatever the Cost*.[2] But this book isn't about why we got *fired*; it's about why we got *hired* in the first place. It's our story of how God's truths applied to our work *actually worked* and put us in the position to have a reality show centered on the company we built.

This book contains the guide we created to help us build multiple businesses across several verticals to achieve financial freedom and independence long before reality TV came knocking on our door.

You see, when HGTV fired us and the media smeared our names through the mud, it didn't affect our income one bit.

---

[2] *Whatever The Cost* (Thomas Nelson, 2015)

Sure, some of our business income took a hit. But personally, *we never missed a beat*. By that time, we were financially free, and there was nothing anyone could say or do that would change that.

Our income was not determined by people liking us. And, as any entrepreneur will tell you, that's a wonderful place to be. It's the place where we want *you* to be—and where you *can* be if you apply the steps we outline in these pages.

So, what is an Expert Owner? At its core, an Expert Owner is someone who views *God as the true owner* of their business, and themselves as *stewards of it*. Because of this, Expert Owners give God the final say over everything they do. With God calling the shots, they view their business not just as a means to generate income but as an engine for impact—a tool through which they can *glorify God and bless people at the same time.*

The Expert Ownership *program* is the twelve-step process we developed to help you become an Expert Owner. It's built upon these three pillars:

- A thriving business
- Financial freedom
- A life of impact

If you want these three things, this program is for you. We're going to show you exactly how we achieved them and how you can, too.

But be warned, we talk about God ... *a lot*. This book pulls no punches. We leave it all on the table. Everything that has brought us success in the world of business and money, we document in these pages. And this is why we talk about God so much: He knows how to run a business and generate wealth better than we do.

We've wanted to write this book for a long time. Over the last decade, it seems like we've said to each other more than a dozen times, "I think now is the time to write our business book." But as each year passed, it became clear that God had a different plan. Fortunately, however, we've learned even more over the last ten years—information you will benefit from in the pages that follow.

It's our mission to help you own all the major aspects of your life. This book will start by showing you how to own your business so it doesn't own you. But, the "*own it*" philosophy doesn't stop there. When it comes to your personal health and well-being - *own it* ...your marriage and family life - *own it* ...your friendships and social life - *own it* ...your faith walk and life's mission - *own it*! Expert Ownership means you are in total command of all 360 degrees of your life...so you get to live life on your terms.

This is why the Expert Ownership program is about more than just helping you with your business. We want you to thrive in *every* area of your life.

We divided the book into two separate parts.

Part One shares the story of how we got our start and the *mindset* that allowed us to build our first business from a tiny two-man shop into a nationwide brand.

Part Two is where we'll spend the bulk of our time. This is where we jump into our twelve-step program—the *method* we developed to build and scale our businesses while managing our money to become SeeYaPreneurs.

You'll see throughout the book that we always talk about *mindsets* before *methods*. If you can get your thinking straight, the doing will always fall into place.

In these pages, we'll take you to our first office, where we got down on our knees every morning and begged God to bring clients our way. You'll ride with us in our little truck as we mowed lawns and painted houses to make extra cash when our business couldn't pay us. You'll tag along on a trip we took with our dad to a restaurant where our only purpose was to watch the busboy. And we'll bring you into our conference room and explain why our table is actually a door.

We're going to show you the principles we discovered in the Bible that will help you build, grow, and sustain your business while not forsaking what you value most—your family and the people you love. We'll show you how to own your business without it owning you. We'll teach you how to leverage the active income from your business to create passive income from your investments.

But most of all, we'll equip and empower you to live out your God-given call in the marketplace.

We did a lot of stuff right. We also did a lot of stuff wrong. There are days we look back and say to ourselves, *what on earth were we thinking?* But one thing we've never questioned was our commitment to follow God as our leader and treat Him as our business partner.

We can't wait to dive in.

AUTHORS' NOTE

Before we get started, let's figure out where you are *right now*.

We've created a chart that maps our journey from wage-slaves to financial freedom. As one of our favorite authors, Robert Kiyosaki, puts it: from employees, to self-employed, to business owners, to investors. *Or*, as *we* like to call them ... from WannaPreneurs, to SoloPreneurs, to Entrepreneurs, and finally, to SeeYaPreneurs.

This chart looks at various aspects of your life and business—such as time, work, money, your customers, systems, and vacation time. It even considers your income ceiling and compares how growing from one stage to the next radically transforms your life. The chart highlights the reason you should never stay stagnant but must continue moving forward to achieve a life of freedom. As you read through it, consider where you are now and where you'd like to one day be.

So, let's start with time ...

- A WannaPreneur (employee) trades time for money.
- A SoloPreneur (self-employed person) also trades time for money ... but there's a chance it's a bit more.
- An Entrepreneur (business owner) trades other people's time for money.
- And a SeeYaPreneur (investor) trades money for money and keeps all his time for himself.

What about work?

- A WannaPreneur has a job and a boss.

- A SoloPreneur has a job and is their own boss.
- An Entrepreneur is the boss.
- And a SeeYaPreneur has no boss and doesn't need to be a boss.

Now, what about customers?

- A WannaPreneur calls the customers.
- A SoloPreneur tries to get customers to call them.
- An Entrepreneur's customers call their team.
- And a SeeYaPreneur has no need for customers (they can live off their assets).

With systems ...

- A WannaPreneur works in the system.
- A SoloPreneur works in and manages the system.
- An Entrepreneur owns the system.
- And a SeeYaPreneur transcends the system.

Now, let's look at our cherished vacation time ...

- A WannaPreneur usually has two weeks *paid*, and you're coming back.
- A SoloPreneur's vacation time is *unpaid*, and you better get back.
- An Entrepreneur might get six weeks of paid vacation, but your team *needs* you back.
- However, a SeeYaPreneur has paid vacation at any time and no one needs you back.

Finally, with your income ceiling ...

- A WannaPreneur's boss determines the ceiling.
- A SoloPreneur's time and effort determine the ceiling.

- An Entrepreneur's system and team determine the ceiling.
- A SeeYaPreneur has no ceiling.

No matter who you are, or where you are on this chart, if you're like us (or most people), it's hard enough to figure out how to survive in the place where you are, much less move to the next level. But what we're about to share with you will show you how.

Are you ready?

	WANNAPRENEURS (EMPLOYEE)	SOLOPRENEURS (SELF-EMPLOYED)	ENTREPRENEURS (BUSINESS OWNER)	SEEYAPRENEURS (INVESTOR)
TIME	Trade time 4 money T = $	Trade your own time for Money T = $$, trade your money for your time (hiring contractors)	Trade Other People's Time for Money P=$$$ (leverage employees)	Trade Money for Money $$$ = $$$$$$
WORK	You have a job and a boss	You have a job but you are your own boss	You are the boss	There is no boss
MONEY	Nobody makes you money	You make the money (When you're there)	People make you money (w/out you there)	Money makes you money
CLIENTS AND CUSTOMERS	Your boss/company chooses your clients	Your clients choose you	You choose your clients (can fire a bad client etc)	You don't need clients
SYSTEM	You're in someone else's system	You manage your system and work in your own system	You own the system and other people work in your system	You transcend systems
VACATION	Two Weeks Paid (you're coming back)	Unpaid (until you can't afford it or something blows up; "workcations")	Paid (until they need you back)	Anytime Paid (don't have to come back)
CEILING	Your boss determines your ceiling	Your time & effort determine your ceiling	Only your systems and team determine your ceiling	There is no ceiling

PART ONE

Our Story

CHAPTER ONE

THE CONFERENCE

The two of us stood in front of a packed room filled with entrepreneurs from around the country. Each had come to be a part of our rapidly expanding company, the Benham Real Estate Group. On the podium in front of us rested three things—the conference agenda, notes for our opening session, and a Bible.

This event marked seven years in business for us. Three years earlier, our little real estate company had grown so fast we'd decided to franchise it, and—with hardly a clue as to what we were doing—we launched out and opened fifty locations in only two years. By the time we held this conference, we had grown to 100 locations across thirty-five states.

The audience that day consisted of a host of current and potential franchisees along with their spouses, business partners, and staff members. Our goals were to …

- Educate them in our business methods
- Equip them with the systems and tools they would need to succeed
- Help them embark on the path to financial freedom
- Engage them to use their business to make an impact for God in their communities

Our conference theme was based on Mark 8:36: "What shall it profit a man if he gains the whole world yet forfeits his soul?" We didn't want to train our franchisees to make money without talking about the importance of them having real meaning in their business and in their personal lives.

We'd seen too many entrepreneurs achieve income and yet have no impact. They earned profit but had no peace. They achieved a version of success, yet it was without any real significance. We didn't want that for the people who had entrusted their lives and businesses to our leadership.

At the close of our opening speech, we asked the crowd to do an exercise with us. This is an activity we've done for years—one that keeps us centered on a vital key to business success: prioritizing relationships over riches. We learned it from Psalms 90:12, which instructs, "Teach us to number our days, that we might gain a heart of wisdom."

We'd like to do this exercise with you right now, right at the outset of this book, just as we did with our franchisees back then.

Imagine you're at your own funeral.

You're lying in a casket and you can see all the people walking by, wiping tears away as they pause to remember you. Your neighbors from down the street, your coworkers, clients, distant relatives, close friends, and some not-so close friends—they're all present to pay their respects. Then your spouse walks by, surrounded by your kids, as they hold each other and cry together.

What's going through your mind at that moment? Are you thinking …

I wish I would've made more money. If only I could've taken more meetings. I wish I had a bigger social media following. If only I had made one more sale …

… or are you thinking…

I wish I would've told my friends how much I appreciated them.

*I should've taken fewer meetings and made it to more of my kids'
ball games. I wish I'd spent as much on date night as I did on client
meetings. My coworkers didn't always see the best of me. I wish I
had shared my faith more.*

Everything going through your mind as you lie there in
your casket has nothing to do with business, money, fame, or
success, does it? It has everything to do with *relationships*. And
the most important of all are your relationships with God and
the people He's put around you.

Now, shift your focus to another scenario.

Imagine that you own a business in Berlin in 1942. Hitler
is in charge and business is booming. One day, you're taking
some clients to golf on a course outside Auschwitz to talk
business when you look up and see smoke rising from an open
field. You and your clients walk over the crest of green to get
a closer look, and you see piles of shoes, mounds of glasses,
books, and even hair. Then, to your horror, you see heaps of
dead bodies dumped on top of each other.

At that moment, what's going through your mind? Are you
thinking ...

*How can I increase my sales next quarter so I can play golf more
often? I need to hurry back to the office so I can wrap up that
project I'm working on. I wonder if my assistant can book me at the
Chophouse tonight.*

... or are you thinking ...

*I can't believe this is happening. I have to do something about it!
I need to use my influence as a business owner to stop this horror. I
need to leverage my resources to help these people.*

You see, there were a lot of successful businesses back in
Hitler's time. There were even big churches with fancy

services. But we're not talking about any of them today. We only remember the faithful heroes who risked everything to stand up for those who couldn't defend themselves, bold leaders who counted the cost and paid a price to stand for what was right.

Our question for you is the same one we asked our franchisees back then: *What are you going to do with the business you've built?* Are you going to use it to "live the good life" ... or are you going to build a business that provides you with a platform to make an impact in your community and help those who cannot help themselves?

You see, this is why we wrote this book. This is why we held that conference. We want to see entrepreneurs crush it in business so they can use those businesses to bless people AND make an impact in the world, to stand for what's good and true and right in the face of evil and darkness.

On the last night of our conference, we hosted a black-tie dinner. Our theme for the evening was based on Proverbs 24:11: "Rescue those being led away to death; hold back those staggering toward slaughter." An odd theme for sure, but we'd seen firsthand in our own business journey the power of an entrepreneur with a mission that pressed beyond the simple accumulation of wealth.

After we smashed some grossly overpriced and not-so-tender fillets, we read a true story that had taken place in Nazi Germany. It told of a German man who was an eyewitness to the atrocity of the Holocaust and his account of why many Germans refused to speak up.

> *"I was a young man living in Germany during the holocaust," the man said. "I considered myself a Christian. I attended a little church with my family from the time I was a small boy. We all heard about the atrocities that were*

happening not far from us in Auschwitz, but it was too difficult to comprehend. What could we do anyway?

"There was a train track behind our church, and week after week we would hear the sound of the whistle and the clacking of the wheels as the train passed. It never bothered us. We grew accustomed to it. One morning we heard noise coming from the train. It was the sound of wailing and moaning. We were shocked when we realized that there were people in those boxcars! They were being led away to death.

"Week after week that train whistle blew, and we heard the sound of those poor Jews crying out. It was so disturbing that we devised a plan. We moved up our [church] song service, so that when the train passed, we would be singing. We sang as loud as we could to drown out the cries. If, perchance, we still heard them, we just sang a little louder.

"Years have passed, and no one talks about it much anymore, but I still hear the sound of that train whistle in my sleep. I can still hear them crying out for help. God forgive me! God forgive all of us who called ourselves Christians, yet did nothing to intervene."[3]

When we finished the story, we took our franchisees back to 1942 as we did with you earlier, encouraging them to use their business to make an *impact*, not just an *income*.

By the time we were done, we could see several people were visibly impacted, sitting in silence as they contemplated a life of success with no real significance. Our hearts burned as we stood in front of them. We could see the Lord stirring the hearts of those who listened. It brought a spiritual adrenaline rush for us to see people view their businesses in a different light.

---

[3] Penny Lea, *Sing A Little Louder*, http://www.internationalwallofprayer.org/A-010-Holocaust-Memorial-Day-Stover.html

It was a powerful moment. But the real impact of that conference happened within. That evening, the two of us felt God whispering this message to our hearts: *This is what I made you boys for. I gave you this platform to help others build businesses that bless people, to strengthen their relationships, and to bring Me glory on the earth.*

Since that night, this has become our mission. We burn with a passion to see good people do great things through business to affect change in culture for the glory of God. The book you hold in your hands is a product of that calling.

We shared this story and did this exercise with you at the outset because we want you to think about why you're in business and how you can use your business for impact. The calling you have as an entrepreneur is an important one. Throughout history, God has raised influential businesspeople to effect positive change in culture. We want to be a part of that. The question is, do you?

We believe you do. It's why you're still reading. So, let's lock arms and walk this entrepreneurial journey together as we strive to become the people of influence God has created us to be.

To kick it off, let's go back to a hospital in Orlando, Florida, where a set of twin boys were about to be born … and their dad was passed out drunk on the waiting room floor.

CHAPTER TWO

BEGINNINGS

Our mom didn't know she was having twins until two days before she was due. Talk about a wake-up call! The real wake-up call, though, was for our dad. At least, the one God was about to give him.

The night we were born, Dad was passed out on the hospital's waiting room floor after an all-night poker party. He owned the Madhatter Saloon in Kissimmee, Florida, where he drank almost as much he sold. Business and beer—those two things were in his blood. His dad, whom we called Grampa, owned the famous Jimmy Benhams in Syracuse, New York.

Grampa's bar was the place to be in the Cuse. His knack for making people smile (coupled with Gramma's prime rib) made it one of the most-frequented bars in town.

That was the life our dad knew. So when he graduated from Florida State University, he did what any entrepreneur's kid would do ... he started a bar of his own.

Business was good, at first. Dad possessed the same charisma and charm as Grampa, which kept a steady flow of customers filtering through the door each night. Although he hadn't taken business courses or followed any ten-step startup plans, his business excelled because he was good at relationships.

We tell aspiring entrepreneurs that the key to making it in business is by mastering relationships. Find someone's pain, alleviate that pain, and make them feel good while you're doing it, and you have found a winning formula in the world of a business owner.

Both Dad and Grampa shined when it came to interacting with people. So Dad had no problem talking with a guy who walked into his bar one day selling coffee makers. Gene was his name. He was a modern-day Apostle Paul. Just as Paul built tents for income and shared the Gospel for impact, Gene sold coffee makers for money but shared his faith to help people find true meaning.

Gene gave Dad the best sales pitch he could that day, but he soon recognized there was something bigger at stake than landing a sale. He saw Dad's need for a Savior. In Paul-like fashion, Gene pivoted his presentation. He stopped talking about the features of his coffee maker and started talking about the benefits of salvation.

Dad was intrigued but not convinced. He had heard it all before from our mom, who grew up a good ol' Southern Baptist in the South. She'd been on him for a while to start going to church with her and our sister, Tracy, who was three years old at the time.

But Dad was far too attached to the two things that had given him his identity up to that point—business and beer. Going to church would have to wait.

WAKE UP CALL

After we came into the picture, Dad spent his days helping Mom take care of us and his evenings at the bar. Maybe it was the fact that he had twin baby boys at home who robbed him of sleep every night (or because his oldest daughter tried to torture them during the day), but Dad found himself staying at the bar long after closing hours. He began drinking more of the product that he sold.

The arguments between our parents worsened as Dad grew more and more absent from our lives. Then one night he came home late, drunk as usual, and Mom greeted him with the words he needed to hear: "Pack your stuff and get out! Me and the kids will be fine without you."

Dad told us later that this was the moment he knew he had to change. Mom's plea coupled with Gene's prodding were the Holy Spirit's way of drawing him to God and setting him straight.

Dad asked what it would take to keep her. Mom told him that if he went to church with her that weekend, she'd give him more time to get his act together. He agreed. So, when Sunday rolled around, off to church he went—Gene's church.

Dad can hardly tell this part of the story without getting choked up. He had visited a few churches with Mom when they dated, but the last time they had gone to church together, he'd fallen asleep and thunked his head on the wood pew so loudly that everyone in the church turned around to see what happened. Mom was so embarrassed, she said she'd never go to church with him again.

But this time was different. Sitting there in Gene's church, they listened to a pastor named Dave Klaridy speak a message so powerful that Dad felt like the man was reading his mail. He sat there, wide awake, not able to move and hardly able to breathe. He felt for the first time a tug on his heart that was unlike anything he'd experienced before.

Although he didn't give his heart to the Lord that Sunday, he kept going to church. A few months and several sermons later, Pastor Dave delivered a message that dropped like a bomb out of Heaven on Dad. In that moment, our father felt that sweet crushing all those who've experienced salvation have felt—the moment you know you're a sinner and there's nothing you can do about it, but you have a Savior who took your punishment to set you free.

Dad went to the altar, bowed his knee, repented of his sins, and made his peace with God.

After the service, Dad told Mom to drive the three of us kids home so he could walk. It was a blistering summer day in Kissimmee, but he didn't care. God had done something in his heart, and all he could do was respond. He cried the entire three-mile walk home, pouring his heart out to the Lord in a way only a broken sinner can do. That was the day of salvation for our dad—the day Jesus entered his heart and set him on a path that would change the trajectory of our family forever.

For the next several months, Dad found himself running his business in a new way—witnessing to everyone who bellied up to the bar. He was now more concerned with the meaning of his life than making money to support it. He knew he had found the answer, and it had nothing to do with running a successful business or staring at the bottom of an empty beer bottle. It had everything to do with being at peace with God and helping others to experience the same.

A few months later, our dad felt God calling him to become a pastor, to take his knowledge of building a business and use it to build a church. Shortly thereafter, he sold the bar, packed up our family of five, and moved to Lexington, Kentucky, where he attended seminary.

Just like that, Dad went from business owner and bartender to Bible school student and budding preacher. God used our mom and Gene to turn his life completely around. Three years later, in July 1980, he planted a church in Dallas, Texas, which met in our house.

The door greeters that first Sunday were two of the most terrorizing four-year-old twin boys you'd ever meet. We were typical preacher's kids (the ones you love to hate). We tied people's shoes together in the middle of prayer, challenged guests' kids to boxing matches in the backyard, laughed hysterically during communion, and did every other annoying thing PKs do.

THE CHURCH BIZ

Regardless of how annoying we might have been as kids, growing up on the leadership side of a church gave us the foundation we needed to run our businesses like Dad led his church—with a heart to help people and to make an impact in the community.

One of the best things he taught us during those years was something he used to say all the time:

"If your theology does not become your biography, then your theology is worthless."

In other words, if your thoughts about God don't transition into the way you live your life and do your work, you're living a lie. That was Dad's motto. He taught us that it didn't matter if we were playing baseball or writing a paper or running a business; our one responsibility was to live out our faith right where God placed us and to strive for excellence in all we did.

But these weren't just words of advice. Our dad lived them out, and sometimes the price was high.

When we were about fourteen years old, ten years after starting the church, Dad told our family that he was moving the church office out of our house into a small commercial space. (Mom seemed more excited about it than he did. With only 1,100 square feet of living space, she was ready to have her living room back.)

"You know why I'm moving my office?" Dad asked us.

We didn't.

"Because it's next door to the busiest abortion clinic in Dallas. We can't grow a church and not do something to help the most defenseless people in our city," he explained. "I can't preach the Bible but not live the Bible. These babies need a voice, and we're about to give them one."

One of the workers at that clinic was Norma McCorvey, who was the "Jane Roe" in the *Roe v Wade* Supreme Court case that legalized abortion in America in January 1973. Two years later Dad moved the church, through his influence and that of a few other key people, she gave her heart to Jesus. Dad baptized her in a backyard swimming pool surrounded by news media from all over the nation.

But being a pastor and an outspoken pro-life advocate was risky back in those days. Few pastors spoke out in that way because it was labeled "political." If they spoke up for unborn babies, it could cost them their church.

And that's exactly what happened. The "powers that be" in the Free Methodist denomination we belonged to felt that Dad couldn't be a pastor and a pro-life activist at the same time, so they removed him from his position.

We watched our dad pay a price for his faith. It cost his reputation, his income, and the church he loved pastoring. Yet he never backed down from standing up for what was right.

Living out his faith and using his organization (our church) to impact culture was the example we had as kids. He operated with a whatever-the-costmindset and was not afraid to lose the organization he led. Our dad's strong convictions played out before our very eyes, and we never forgot it.

Years later, when our reputations and organization were on the line for our Christian values, it was this very example that pulled us through. We learned that real faith was not just something to talk about on Sundays but to live out every day.

COMMUNITY IS KEY

Our dad wasn't the only one who impacted us during our younger years and gave us the foundation we needed to launch out as entrepreneurs and build businesses. God raised up several other men who played vital roles in shaping us for our future.

These men showed us firsthand that *success in business paves the way for you to bless people in a great way.* Their example lodged deep in our hearts, and the generosity we saw in them became a burning passion of ours as we began to experience business success.

Shortly after Dad lost his position in the church, the two of us boys were playing catch in the street when a family friend, Mr. Dave White, pulled up in his Mercedes Benz with Dad in the passenger seat. Dad got out with a shoebox in his hand, walked over to us, and lifted the lid. Inside were the nicest, most expensive dress shoes we'd ever seen. Mr. Dave, like a lot of other successful businessmen, was a "shoe guy," and he didn't want to buy himself a pair without getting our dad a new pair as well.

It may seem like a petty thing, but at the time it spoke volumes to all of us—that Mr. Dave cared enough to put the finest shoes money could buy on a pastor who was sidelined for standing true to his convictions. He did it for several years after that, and it became a tradition Dad always looked forward to. Dave's generosity etched in our hearts a passion to one day be in a position to do the same.

Richard Couron was another man who had a lasting impact on our lives. He and his family started coming to church when it was held in our house. We didn't know it at the time, but Richard was a serial entrepreneur who owned a leading tech company that was uber successful. You'd never know it by the modest house he had or the van he drove. (Admittedly, we were a little jealous of the Zodiac shoes and Z. Cavaricci pants his sons, David and Ricky, wore. If you grew up in the '80s, you know wearing those brands meant you had *arrived*. Maybe that's why all the girls liked them more than us.) *(Jason:Actually, I think it was David's chili-bowl haircut that turned them away)*.

Richard was good to our family throughout his time in the church. A little gift here. A little check there. He was devastated when Dad got the ax, but he also saw God's hand leading Dad into full-time pro-life work. Wanting to make sure Dad could stay there without feeling the heavy financial pressure of raising a family, he put him on his payroll.

Who does that?

Richard showed us what a God-fearing, Gospel-loving entrepreneur can do and the lives he can impact by being good at his work and generous with his profit. We cannot even begin to count the number of babies that have been saved because of our dad's presence at abortion clinics across America. But the unsung hero was the man who helped keep him there—a godly entrepreneur with a heart that burned for the Lord.

Here's the cool part: Richard kept Dad on his payroll until the day our business could take over in supporting Dad's ministry.

Both Mr. Dave and Richard are dead and gone now, but their legacies live on. While our dad showed us what faithfulness looked like as a pastor, these men showed us what faithfulness looked like as entrepreneurs and how excellence in business paves the way for impact in life.

As much as we found ourselves wanting to be like our dad *spiritually*, we found ourselves wanting to be like those men *financially*. We didn't thirst for money, but we wanted the ability to bless people in big ways and to get behind godly initiatives like they did. (Maybe we wanted to be able to afford some Zodiacs and Z. Cavariccis too.)

God used these men, along with our dad, to deposit the seeds of faithfulness in our hearts that would one day germinate and grow. Dad showed us how to build, grow, and lead an organization, and then to hold it loosely so that it wouldn't become an idol. While his church was obviously a nonprofit, the principles we learned translated perfectly into the for-profit space.

Mr. Dave and Richard showed us the vast potential of resources generated from owning a successful organization. They demonstrated the power of owning a business that blesses people, impacts communities, and even changes a culture.

But God didn't stop there. He brought one more man into our lives just before we graduated from college who inspired us in our business journey in ways we could never have imagined.

CHAPTER THREE

BOLD IN BUSINESS

In our book *Bold and Broken,*[4] we shared the story of a wealthy businessman who inspired us so much that simply meeting him changed the trajectory of our lives. David Drye was the first person we saw run his business as a ministry—not just with his profits but also with his process. It motivated us to operate in the same way when we started our company years later.

We met him in the fall of 1997, when we were juniors at Liberty University. We had just spent Thanksgiving in Atlanta, Georgia, with our extended family. Over Thanksgiving break, our dad told us about a real estate magnate he wanted us to meet.

"His name is David Drye, and he's doing amazing things for the Lord," Dad said. "He flew me in to speak to his company and the school he started."

Mr. Drye was a successful businessman who not only ran a company but operated a Christian school and hosted a Christian television show. He lived in Concord, North Carolina, which just so happened to be on our way back from Atlanta to Liberty University in Virginia. When Dad told him we'd be passing through, he invited the two of us to spend the night at his house on Sunday and then speak to his team and at his school on Monday morning.

---

[4] *Bold and Broken* (Salem Books, 2019)

We showed up that Sunday night and quickly realized our dad had seriously underplayed Mr. Drye's business success. From the enormity of his house and the size of his property, it was clear he experienced a level of financial success beyond anything we'd ever seen.

As we gaped at each other in amazement, we could tell what we both were thinking. Our first thought was, *What kind of business does this guy have, and how can we get involved?*

We walked up the brick steps to the porch, where we were greeted by a man in his fifties who beamed with excitement. "I'm so glad you guys are here," he said. "Come in and meet my family."

We had never been in a house quite like that in all our lives. We made the effort to stop gasping at the magnitude of the place and noticed a bunch of kids sitting on couches in the living room, eating. He introduced them as the five youngest of his eight children.

"You guys want a Mr. C's burger?" he asked. "These things are famous around here."

Asking a couple of starving college guys if they would like to eat burgers is like asking if fat puppies like big bones. Basically, there's no need to ask.

After indulging in a few Mr. C's burgers and confirming they were worthy of the "famous" tag, we followed Mr. Drye upstairs. He put us in his boys' room for the night, just down the hall from his office. We were bummed we had to take the stairs instead of the elevator—apparently, he wanted us to get a workout.

"Breakfast is at 7:00 a.m.," he said. "We've got a big day planned for tomorrow."

As we lay there in the darkened silence of that room, we quietly marveled at how successful this man was. We didn't run in circles with people like this.

WAKE UP!

We drifted off to sleep in the amazing beds whose comfort far exceeded the twin-sized mattresses back at our Liberty dorm room. Then, at 4:30 a.m., we were startled awake by the sound of someone yelling down the hall.

Jumping out of bed, we both got up and crept to the door. Cracking it open, we peered down the long dark hallway. We could see light coming out from under the door of Mr. Drye's office. As we stood there with hearts pounding, we realized he wasn't yelling …

David Drye was praying.

For the next hour, we heard him pour his heart out to the Lord and do battle with the enemy. He would go from telling God how much he loved Him to rebuking the devil in the name of Jesus. "You have no authority over my family or my business, Devil!" he shouted. "Get away from them!"

We had grown up in a family that believed in prayer and put that belief into practice. But this was a whole new level—never before had we seen such emphatic prayer. This man sounded like he was locked in a hand-to-hand combat with the devil.

Fortunately, we were able to fall back asleep for about an hour. Then we crawled out of bed, washed up, and headed downstairs to talk to our newfound prayer-warrior/business-tycoon buddy.

"We heard you praying early this morning," we told Mr. Drye.

"Oh. Sorry about that," he said. "I go to war on my knees before I start my day, or I don't feel right."

We polished off breakfast and then were whisked away in his Suburban, heading to his office where we were set to speak to his staff. On the way, we asked him to tell us the story of how he started his business.

"I began in insurance," he said. "But then I realized I wanted to create something that could make millions of dollars to fund God's work on the earth. So I got into real estate."

Whoa. We had never heard anyone talk like that before. A person who wanted to make millions of dollars to give away!?

Before we could ask any further questions, we pulled up to a big white building with the words "David Drye Company" on the marquee out front. We walked into the foyer and up the stairs to a large conference room where about thirty people were gathered, waiting for Mr. Drye—and us.

This guy has thirty employees? That's huge! We were impressed, but then found out these people were only a few of his leaders and support staff. His company employed nearly four hundred people, who managed his forty-three apartment complexes across three states.

We spent the whole day with Mr. Drye as he hauled us from one speaking engagement to the next. The longer we were with him, the more impressed and inspired we became. We probably asked him no fewer than 100 questions. We couldn't drive more than two or three miles without him pointing out another apartment complex he owned, or a fun park he had opened, or an office complex he had built.

The whole time, he explained that his entire business was built upon prayer. "I have prayed for the last twenty years that God would bless my business," he said. "I shout, '*God, bust those*

*rocks and break those chains that hold back Your blessing from me.
I commit my way to You. Give me more that I may bless You with
it!'* Boys, God has answered my prayers."

While he was talking, his fists were balled up and swinging
wildly. He was a very passionate guy. And he had no idea
how to wait until his truck came to a complete stop before he
changed gears. He'd back out of a parking spot at warp speed
and slam it into drive before he even pushed the brake. It was
an adventurous ride that day—in more ways than one.

At the end of the day, as we were driving back to his house,
he asked if we would mind flying back to Liberty in his
helicopter since he didn't have time to drive us back.

Ummm, are you kidding? we thought. *That might just make
us the most popular dudes at LU! (Jason: David needed some
help moving up the popularity scale.)* We had never been in a
helicopter before.

THE MISSION

When we pulled onto the half-mile-long driveway leading to
his house, Mr. Drye reached into his pocket and pulled out a
small, worn piece of paper. "Do you boys know what this is?"
he asked.

"No, sir," we answered.

"On this sheet of paper," he continued, "I've written goals for
my family and my business. When you guys heard me this
morning, I was laying my hands on these goals and asking
God to help me accomplish everything on the list. But I know
Satan doesn't want me to succeed, so when I pray, I know I've
entered a battlefield in the spiritual realm. I wage war in the
spirit before I go to war in business."

As he was talking, he handed us the piece of paper.

"Take a look," he said. "I want you to see what I've written on there. I don't usually do this, but I feel the Lord wants me to let you see it."

We couldn't get past the first point: *Give away $1 million a month from my business.*

We had never seen a number like that before, much less seen it written down as a specific goal and prayed over by a man who was well on his way to accomplishing it.

He looked at us with penetrating eyes. "Boys, I believe God has a great plan for both of you. But that plan is only going to go as far as your prayer life is deep. You need to go after God in prayer like never before. Make big goals for yourselves, spiritually and financially, and then go after them until He either grants your request or gives you something else to ask for."

When we handed the paper back to him, he asked us something we totally unexpected. "When baseball is over, would you consider coming to work for me? I've been praying for God to spark a revival in America right here from Concord, and I want to pour myself into young men like you, teaching you everything I know."

Uh, do bears poop in the woods? We responded with an emphatic "Yes!"

David Drye had given us a vision for life after baseball: to be part of a thriving business led by a man with a heart to change the world for Christ.

Just before we left, he opened the back door of his Suburban, reached into one of several boxes inside, and handed us each a copy of *The Autobiography of George Müller*. "Aside from the

Bible, this is the best book I've ever read," he told us. "I give them out to everyone I can. I have modeled my prayer life after this great man, and you should too."

Müller's claim to fame was that he built an orphanage in England in the 1800s solely through the power of prayer. He committed to never asking anyone for money to help with his projects; when he needed funds, he would ask God alone. His little orphanage, which started with just a few orphans in one house, grew to thousands in a sprawling campus of houses—all because he partnered with God in his business.

Inside each book was Mr. Drye's business card. The front of the card simply read "Jesus Loves You" in big red letters. On the back was his contact information. It was a simple way to let people know what was most important in his life.

We prayed together and then said goodbye.

Our heads were buzzing on the flight back to Liberty—not just because we were stoked to be flying in a helicopter but because we felt our future had just opened up for us in a way neither of us had foreseen.

ETERNAL IMPACT

Our prayer lives changed that day, as did our idea of business. Mr. Drye showed us how those things work together—how his prayers fueled his business, and his resultant success in business gave him more time to pray.

We also read the book by Müller. It's a must-read for anyone who wants God as a business partner.

A year later, the two of us were drafted into professional baseball—David by the Red Sox and me (Jason) by the Orioles. In my second year as a minor leaguer for the Orioles,

I broke my leg in Hickory, North Carolina, less than an hour from where Mr. Drye lived. We tell the details in our book *Miracle in* Shreveport.[5] It was an epic break, one that required emergency surgery and several days in the hospital.

Because it was the final game of a seven-day road trip, our team couldn't wait for me, so they left me behind and headed home. By the time I got out of surgery, I was stuck in Hickory, alone in a hospital room.

The next morning, after I finished breakfast, I heard a knock at the door. "Come in," I called, wondering who in the world it could be. To my total amazement, it was David Drye along with one of his sons. We hadn't seen each other in two years.

He stepped into the hospital room. "We heard about what happened to you and we came to pray for your healing," he said. A huge smile crossed his face. "You didn't think you could be so close to us and I wouldn't come see you, did you?"

"How did you hear?" I asked.

"Your dad called last night to ask for prayer," he said. "So I told him I would do even better—I'd come pray for you in person."

I was thankful to see a familiar face. I was even more thankful it was a man who prayed like him.

As we talked together, he gave out his "Jesus Loves You" business card to every nurse or doctor who came into the room. Then he placed one in the picture frame on the wall in front of my bed. I looked at that thing every day I was in the hospital and thanked God for a man like David Drye.

---

[5] *Miracle in Shreveport* (Thomas Nelson, 2018)

After we prayed together, I said, "I just gotta ask—did you fly your helicopter here?"

He flashed that grin once again. "Yep. Landed it on the roof."

He then asked if I'd read the book on George Müller. I told him I had and how it was definitely worth the recommendation. He said he'd send me a case full of them so I could give them to the guys on my team.

"Don't forget," he said as he and his son got up to leave, "I want you and David to move to Concord and work with me when baseball is over."

"That's a deal," I said.

He leaned over and hugged me. After he walked out of the room, I was struck with the feeling that this was one of the greatest human beings I had ever met. I remember thinking it would be nice to be like him one day.

One month later, I was recovering at my parents' house in Dallas when we got a phone call.

"David Drye and his wife, Ann, were just killed in a plane crash," said the voice on the other end of the line.

I lost my breath.

They had been traveling in his private plane, headed to their beach house, when one of the engines failed. The pilot almost made it back to the runway, but their wing clipped a tree and the plane flipped upside down. One of the company's senior members had also been on the plane. No one survived.

I couldn't believe what I heard. *There's no way—just no way he's gone.* My mind was racing in a million directions. I had put so much hope into a future with Mr. Drye, learning what it meant to be a successful businessman operating according to biblical principles ... and now he was gone.

Two days later, while I was still in shock from that phone call, I received a package from Concord. I opened it, and there was the case of George Müller books Mr. Drye had promised to send. On top was a scribbled note in his handwriting:

"Have fun giving these out. Let's talk soon—David Drye."

Tears welled up in my eyes and I could barely keep it together. He had mailed that box to me before he boarded the plane that day. One of the last things he had done on this earth was to send me a box of faith-building books I could give out to others—to share the testimony of a man who lived by faith and ran his business by the power of prayer.

I placed one of the copies on my bookshelf. I still have it today. It serves as a constant reminder, not just of the prayer-warrior minister the book is about but also of the prayer-warrior businessman who gave it to me. He modeled what true success in business means.

THE PERFECT PLACE TO LAUNCH

Two years later, in 2001, when baseball was all over for me, my wife and I moved to Concord and I took a job as the ministry coordinator for the David Drye Company. It was a position Mr. Drye had created before his death with a two-fold purpose: to serve as both chaplain for the employees and outreach coordinator for the community. When David got out of baseball the next year in 2002, he moved his young family here and took a job as the janitor at David Drye'sschool. Later that year, the rest of our family—Mom, Dad, our brother and two sisters, and our in-laws—moved to Concord.

But with the vacancy of Mr. Drye's leadership, the company

he had created began to flounder. Many employees were laid off, including the two of us. In January 2003, we found ourselves jobless and clueless about what to do next. All we knew was that we wanted to make an impact *somehow, some way,* just as David Drye had done. But what direction were we supposed to go?

We needed some guidance—and quick. Because the two of us were about to launch out in the wrong direction.

CHAPTER FOUR

THE CALL

From the time we were teenagers, the two of us knew we'd always work together. It just seemed like the thing to do. That, and our parents reminded us that God made us twins for a reason, and it wasn't so we could go our separate ways.

We also assumed we'd become full-time ministers when baseball was over. Maybe it was the influence of our dad, or all the amazing speakers we heard in chapel while at Liberty University. We respected and admired those who helped lead people into deeper relationships with God. We believed that we would be called to do the same thing in our vocation.

Then we met Mr. Drye, and he opened our eyes to a whole new world of possibility. But when his company began to fold after his death, we found ourselves jobless in that freezing cold January of '03. So we figured that was God's way of moving us back into the direction of full-time ministry. We talked with several close friends and family members about it and all of them agreed: "You boys were made to be in the ministry."

Armed with a calling for ministry and confirmation from those who knew us best, we started Benham Brothers Ministries with the goal of using our background in professional sports to tell people about Jesus. We built a website, got some marketing material together, and even wrote a letter seeking financial support.

Just before we mailed it, we decided to pray over it and dedicate our new ministry to the Lord. We got down on our knees, just like David Drye had modeled, and asked God to bless our efforts. But as we began to pray, God impressed upon our hearts that we weren't supposed to send the letter to anyone. It was an odd feeling, like a discomfort that maybe we weren't going in the right direction.

The more we prayed, the stronger the feeling grew: We didn't need to send the letter. Even more, we felt like God wanted us to rip it up.

We were taken aback. It didn't make sense. Yet as we prayed, God made it clear that raising support was a valid model for *some* people, but it wasn't the model for us. As we understood it, that meant we'd have to put our goal of being "in the ministry" on hold.

Of course, our idea of ministry was off. What we didn't realize then but now know is that we were *already* ministers. We learned that where we're placed and how we're paid doesn't determine the ministry. What makes a minister is God's presence in our lives and our passion to glorify Him through our work. We could be full-time ministers right where we were no matter what we did for a living, and that included owning a business. We'll talk about this more in Chapter Eight.

It would be several years before we came to that realization. At the time, our biggest problem wasn't that we were confused about what ministry was, but that we had young families to support. David was married with two young boys and another child on the way, and I was married with one son and a daughter in the oven. And since neither of us had made it to the Big Leagues, money was in short supply. We had no clue what we would do to earn a living.

Over the next few days, we talked—and prayed—a lot. I (David) had a thought that kept popping into my head as I prayed. Each time I'd ask God, "How am I going to provide for my family?" I'd hear the same question:

What's in your bag?

*I*t reminded me of when Jesus told His disciples to feed the huge crowd of 5,000-plus, and they responded like I did: *Uh, how are we going to feed that many people?* Christ responded, *Well, what do you have?* They didn't have much—only a couple of tuna fish sandwiches. But they were willing to give what little they had, and Jesus performed a mighty miracle with it.[6]

Jason and I didn't have much in our bags. We had both earned history degrees from Liberty, but they were useless because we didn't want to teach. And our baseball experience didn't help much because we didn't want to coach.

The one thing we did have was a pair of real estate licenses. We'd earned those a few months earlier. No, we hadn't planned to go into real estate or anything. I simply wanted to buy a house for my family, as did Jason, and neither of us wanted to pay a commission to an agent. (That's good reasoning, right?)

So that's the direction we chose to go. We figured if Jesus could do something amazing with a few loaves and some fish, He could certainly do something with a couple of young dudes with real estate licenses. We changed Benham Brothers Ministriesto Benham Enterprises, joined a local real estate firm, and started selling houses in February 2003.

Our first business was born.

PRAYING FOR A MIRACLE

We learned two things quickly as full-time real estate agents:

    1. We only made money when we sold houses (no salary = 100 percent commission!).

---

[6] This paraphrased story is found in all four gospels—Matthew 14, Mark 6, Luke 9, and John 6.

2. We were not cut out for B-to-C business (business to consumer).

On the commission front, we found ourselves strapped for income. We literally had ZERO dollars coming in the door, and the constant encouragement from other agents that "it takes time to build your base" wasn't enough to calm that frustration. Never the type to just sit around waiting, we took any odd job we could find.

We mowed lawns, painted houses, trimmed bushes, washed and detailed cars; it didn't matter what it was. If we could make money fast, we did it. We remember taking a job to stain wood doors at an office for eight dollars an hour. We accidentally let a drip run down one of the doors and it dried, and we couldn't get it off. But hey, we were cheap labor!

Fortunately, we still had our little white truck from back in college. It was like we were teenagers again, driving that Isuzu pickup to our next job. Only this time, we had little mouths to feed!

At the same time, we were working hard to get our little real estate business off the ground. We rode around with other agents to learn the ropes, took phone duty, showed houses, went to sales meetings, watched training videos—whatever we were told to do, we did it.

In working with consumers, we learned quickly that the B-to-C model still wasn't up our alley. We would show up to sales meetings in gym clothes and sneakers covered with grass from having just mown a lawn or three, while everyone else was dressed to the nines.

And then there were the "caravans" (the two-hour carpool trip that agents took each week to see the firm's newly listed houses). We'd walk into a house, and the other agents—most of whom were retirement-age women with thick Southern accents—would brag about the contour of the cabinetry and the color of the linen drapes and the softness of the nylon carpet. Meanwhile all we were thinking was, *When will this be over and what's in the fridge?*

When it was our turn to show houses to prospective buyers, we'd walk into a house and know within twenty seconds if they were going to buy it or pass. The two of us were all about the transaction, not the emotion. The husband would be moseying around the backyard while the wife strolled leisurely through the house, and all the while we would be thinking, *We need to hurry and wrap this up cuz we've got some lawns to mow.* We learned pretty quickly that that type of attitude doesn't fly with customers.

At that point, we realized that if God didn't bring us some other niche in real estate, we were going to have to jump ship. We decided to start going to the office early every day to pray and ask God to open a door for us.

Specifically, we asked God to help us get in with banks to sell their foreclosed houses. We had met an agent from another company who was doing this very thing. He told us that selling houses for banks was better than traditional real estate because you work with a business rather than a consumer. This meant our working hours would be bank hours (i.e., we wouldn't have to show houses at night or on weekends, giving us more time with family).

Also, the sales process was handled as a transaction, not an emotion. This was music to our ears, so we targeted our prayers for God to open a door for us in that niche. Fueled by the examples of David Drye and George Müller, we got down on our knees each morning and begged God to move on our behalf.

It was during those times, down on our knees in desperation, that we remembered how George Müller refused to ask anyone for money to help with his orphanage but vowed to make his financial requests to God alone. In his autobiography, he told a story of when he and the orphans sat at the table for dinner even though there was no food to serve. In faith, he prayed that God would miraculously provide, and in the middle of his prayer someone knocked on the door. A bread truck had broken down in front of the orphanage. Since all the bread would go stale in a few hours, the driver thought he'd give it all to the orphans.[7]

We figured if God did that for Müller, maybe He'd do it for us.

Two weeks went by. Nothing happened.

Then, out of the blue, we got a phone call. I (Jason) was on phone duty taking calls from prospective buyers at the time.

"You don't sell foreclosed properties, do you?" the voice on the other line said.

"Uh, yessir. We do," I responded. At that point, we'd sell matchbox cars or dollhouses or whatever else he needed to get rid of. "We can sell anything you've got."

"This is Bill Spooner from Cloister Bank in Texas. I've got three properties in your area that I need to fix up and sell fast."

"We'll take 'em!" I said before he could say another word.

"Don't you want to see them first?" Bill asked. "I had a few other agents in your area already turn 'em down. They're junk houses."

"Nope!" I said. "We don't care what they look like. We'll take 'em."

---

[7] *The Autobiography of George Müller* (Whitaker House, 1996).

"Well, that's fantastic," he said. "I'll email you the paperwork right now. You have seven days to complete the tasks on the list. When those are done, we'll be in business."

"Thank you very much, Bill," I said, my heart pounding out of my chest from excitement. "If you don't mind me asking, how did you know to call this company?"

"Well," he responded. "I was flipping through the Yellow Pages and I put my finger on this spot. I called the number and you answered."

Prayer answered, George Müller style.

UNDER-PROMISE. OVER-DELIVER.

We were so excited that God answered our prayer that we vowed to blow Bill's hair back with our level of service (assuming he had hair). The only problem was that we didn't have a clue what we were doing.

When we received his list of tasks, it was like reading hieroglyphics. (Thank God Google was already a thing.) After a few searches on "how to sell bank-owned properties," we hopped in the car and sped over to each house, jumping feet-first into the deep end.

We had to check occupancy, rekey the doors if vacant, measure the house, take pictures, get contractor bids for cleanup and repair, schedule utility connection and yard maintenance, get tax information, and perform a full market analysis with our opinion of price. Seven days was the deadline.

With a little help from a contractor friend who owed us a favor, we divided and conquered. Four hours later we had completed every task on all three properties.

Still out of breath from all the hustle, we submitted everything to Bill that day ... and prayed. *God, please help this to be right. And if it's not, can You somehow change it before he looks at it?* That's what we call the prayer of faith in business!

Thirty minutes later, the office phone rang. It was Bill.

"Hello," I (Jason) said, hoping he wasn't mad about some stupid mistake we'd made.

"You have got to be kidding me!" he said excitedly, sounding like a kid opening a present at Christmas. "Never in all my years have I seen agents work this fast! If you guys keep this up, I'll give you every house I've got in your area."

Hearing him say that was like hearing the famous bell in *Rocky III*. (You know, when Rocky was on the mat about to lose to Clubber Lang, and he heard the bell in his head that signified he was about to kick Lang's butt. Yeah, that bell. It was on.)

We knew we had hit something big. Now if we could only find a way to get in with other banks, we could make this new niche into a legitimate business.

But seeing God answer our prayers in this way showed us that He was willing to partner with us in our business. We felt His smile in that moment as He gave us the green light to pursue this niche with every ounce of energy we could muster. It was as if we were two thoroughbreds on race day, and God had just opened the gates and yelled, "RUN!"

And so, we ran. At warp speed.

We told every agent in our area that they no longer had to deal with the headaches of selling bank-owned homes, and that we'd pay a referral if they'd send them to us. Word spread fast, and so did the number of houses. In short order—like three months—we were sitting on fifteen houses for three banks. A few months after that, we had twenty houses for five banks.

That was in 2003, a few years before the floor fell out on the housing industry. We had no clue that a tsunami of foreclosures was about to hit the market. But God knew. And He divinely positioned us to be there when it happened.

All we knew was that we were quickly learning how to specialize in selling the houses nobody else wanted to sell. The successful agents didn't want to stoop down to work with banks. Typically, bank-owned houses were not the nicest on the block. But for us, working with junk properties was a big step up from mowing lawns!

Our pitch to the banks was that we would get done in hours what would take other agents days to do. They'd typically give us a shot (probably laughing under their breath). But when we delivered, their tune changed. Each time they'd send a property, we felt that same shot of adrenaline we experienced when we connected on an inside fastball that we laced over the fence. *(David: I had quite a few more of those than Jason.)* *(Jason: Not true.)*

And things got even better. Not only did God walk us into a business-to-business situation that alleviated the need to show houses, attend sales meetings, or ride in that gawd-awful caravan again, He gave us an opportunity to make money outside of commission. Since each house needed cleaning, lawn maintenance, and repairs, we were able to do the work ourselves while we waited for the house to sell. Cha-ching.

That first year, we brought in $39,946 ... to split. A modest beginning, but our little business was growing. During that time, we held onto this little saying: "Pennies make dollars." Selling bank-owned homes was hard work for little profit, but we knew we were onto something. And while we were focused on making as many pennies as we could, God was giving us the foundation we needed to start making dollars ... lots of them.

CHAPTER FIVE

PARTNERING WITH GOD

About a month after we got our first few properties from Bill, we started scouring the internet for other banks that had foreclosed houses. We discovered there was an entire industry under the umbrella term "REO" (real estate owned) that was primed and ready for us to take over. REO is the term on a bank's balance sheet for houses they own due to foreclosure.

Banks don't want to be in the housing business; they want to be in the money business. So they hire agents, auction companies, and outsource groups to manage and sell those houses. We just needed to get our feet in the door of that niche … somehow.

While searching online for openings, we discovered that one of the biggest banks in the country was having a conference at the Interlocken Resort in Keystone, Colorado, and it was open to real estate agents. The only problem was the expense. The registration fee was $1,000, flights were $500 a ticket, a room at the resort was $350 a night, and we'd have to get a rental car. As much as we wanted to go, we were two guys on the verge of moving our families into the same house together (more on that later), and we just couldn't afford it.

You've probably heard the saying, "Where God guides, He provides." Well, it's true. When our grandma heard about our new business venture, she was really excited. She told us that Grampa, who had died several years prior, would be so proud of us for starting our own business. Having run a business herself, she knew there were plenty of upfront costs to get a company off the ground. And she showed up one day with a check for $10,000!

"Grampa would want you guys to have this," she said with a big smile on her face. "He invested money from our business so we could do things like this for our kids and grandkids. I hope it helps you get started."

Help us!? We were absolutely floored by her generosity. She had no idea how badly we needed that money. We promised her we would put it to good use and make Grampa proud.

That $10,000 not only got us out to the conference, but became the seed money we needed to start our business.

We booked our flights, paid the registration, and reserved the finest hotel room money could buy - at the Super 8 motel half an hour away! There was no way we were going to pay $350 a night at a fancy resort.

We flew into Denver late at night, drove our economy rental car to the Super 8 outside Keystone, and prayed for God to help us build our little business into something special.

The two of us woke early the next morning, pulled the curtains back, and saw the amazing Rocky Mountains in all their glory. The sun was hidden behind the peaks, but the rays of light were peering through, beaming in brilliant colors. It was a breathtaking sight. We got down on our knees and asked God to bless our efforts in Keystone and to open doors for us to meet bank asset managers who could give us houses to sell.

We knew the odds were stacked against us. Large banks like the one hosting the conference already had a massive list of real estate agents to handle their portfolios of properties. But we were hopeful. And as we stared out our window at those incredible mountains, we felt God's power. *If God could make the Rocky Mountains,* we thought, *He could certainly build our business.*

We jumped in our tiny rental car and sped over to the Interlocken resort. The parking lot was packed with cars, most of them luxury vehicles. Just before we got out, we prayed again. Only this time, we heard God speak directly to our hearts:

You focus on My thing. I'll focus on your thing.

We knew what that meant - God didn't want us to go in there with the goal of making money, but with a heart to do ministry. We'd been at too many events with Dad where he taught us to get into conversations with people so we could share our faith and witness to them about God's goodness. The thing is, as teenagers, we rarely wanted to do it. The same was true as we sat there in that rental car.

Our whole goal for being at the conference was to learn the REO business and to meet asset managers who could send us houses. That was it. And now God was telling us to lay that down and just focus on witnessing to people?

Uh, OK.

Neither of us were overly excited about the idea, but we also had a lifetime of experiences through which God had proven Himself faithful to us and our family. So we agreed together that our focus would be *ministry* over *money*, and off we went.

We walked in to find the place completely packed—to the tune of about five thousand people. We had absolutely no clue what we were doing, who we would talk to, or what in the world was even going on. All we knew was that the blue brick Nokia phones in our pockets desperately needed the phone numbers of asset managers, yet God had told us *not* to focus on that.

We sat in the opening session, then jumped from break-out session to break-out session until lunch. When lunchtime came, we strolled through the buffet line with two plates each, heaping them with salmon, chicken, steak, and anything else we could find. It had been such a long morning, we felt kind of like we had just broken out of prison and hadn't eaten fine food in ten years. (Although our minor league baseball days were over, we still had Major League appetites.)

We found an empty table in the back and sat down. A few minutes later, as the room started to fill with people, two of the nicest older women came and sat next to us. They talked to us like we were their grandsons. They got a kick out of seeing how much food we were eating.

We sat there and talked for about thirty minutes. They told us about their kids and grandkids and all the fun stuff they did with them. They asked us about our kids and where we had grown up and what life was like as twins. We ultimately got around to sharing our faith, and they pleasantly nodded. While unsure as to what they really thought about us as we smashed our massive plates of food, we felt confident that we were following through on what the Lord had urged us to focus on.

As the conversation turned to business, they asked us where we lived and what we did in the REO industry.

"We're from North Carolina," we said. "And we're real estate agents."

"Oh!" one of them responded. "We're both asset managers, and the state we're over is North Carolina. Maybe we can send you guys some business!"

Come on! In a room of five thousand people, what were the chances of us sitting next to not just one asset manager, but two who covered the very state in which we worked? Only

God could do something like that.

Those two ladies ended up sending us business—lots of it. And they told their asset manager friends about us, too. That single conversation made us well over half a million dollars in revenue over the next several years.

That's the beauty of partnering with God in your business. You can trust Him, and when you do, you won't just be reading stories of George Müller or the Benham brothers ... you'll be creating your own! You'll live your own stories of how your faith intersected with God's faithfulness and you saw powerful transformation in your life and business.

And it will encourage you to continue to be faithful to Him.

The best part of all, when you make God your business partner, He downloads the exact strategy you need to be successful in your endeavor. It will never be a cookie-cutter approach, because God is in the business of doing new things in new ways with people who are willing to trust Him all the way.

A STRATEGIC PARTNER

The more properties that came our way, the clearer things became for how to systematize our process and streamline our workflow so we could scale our operations and grow fast. God would literally wake us up in the middle of the night with ideas on how to organize ourselves and simplify tasks so others could do them as well as (or even better than) we could.

I (Jason) was in charge of creating our system. When I decided to move us from our simple Excel spreadsheet setup to an online application, I vividly remember waking up many nights with "If ... then" logic running through my brain: *If this happens, then this should happen.*

For those who are not familiar with computer logic, it's built on understanding how certain inputs will give you certain outputs. You can't build an online system without this understanding. I happen to be the most technologically illiterate human being on the planet, and yet I knew we couldn't scale our business without this system. And since we were flat broke, we couldn't afford to hire someone to walk us through it.

So, for that brief period of my life, God literally turned my brain into a system-building machine. Yeah, I read some books and studied up on the subject, but there's no way I actually could have *understood* coding syntax and computer programming if God didn't step in and give me the ability to comprehend it. You have no idea how dull I am with anything technical. *(David: Uh, I do. Didn't you get an 820 on the SAT?) (Jason: Zip it!)*

Now, nearly two decades later, I've forgotten all the technicalities of online programming I knew back then. But during that time, God taught me how to be a *systems thinker* ... and with that knowledge, we were able to create a framework for systems development that we call our 4S Model.

But I'm getting ahead of myself. We'll be diving into systems in a later chapter.

In short, we learned during this time that what God orders, He pays for—and we could take that to the bank.

During those first few years of our business, we saw firsthand how involved God would be in our day-to-day operations if we simply let Him. So, every morning before we started our day, we'd get down on our knees in the small office we shared and ask God to bless our efforts.

We prayed for *everything*. We'd ask Him to open doors to new business, give us ingenious ideas on how to scale and better serve our clients, bring good people to us, and show us if we were displeasing Him in any way. We asked Him to help us reach our financial goals and keep people away from us who didn't have our best interests at heart. Nothing was off limits. If it was important enough to worry about, it was important enough to pray about.

As our company grew and we began hiring people, we kept this tradition alive. Several of our new employees even joined us. At the beginning of each day, about half a dozen of us would get on our knees and pray. Doing this was a way of letting our team know we were simply the managing partners of a business. *God was the owner.*

And the more we grew, the more we realized He was the best business partner we could ever ask for!

By the second year, our revenue more than doubled. And in the third year, God took the lid off completely. We sold more foreclosed houses that year than any other agent in the state. We even found ourselves in the market to buy an office for our rapidly growing company … and the building we bought was the very one where the two of us had stained doors three years prior.

Remember that door with the drip? It now serves as a table in our conference room—a constant reminder of our humble beginnings and our ever-faithful business partner.

The only question now was how could we grow even bigger? To find the solution, we turned to the one state in the U.S. where everything is bigger … and better!

CHAPTER SIX

EXPANDING TO THE LONE STAR STATE

You can take the boys out of Texas, but you can't take Texas out of the boys. Growing up in the Lone Star State made us Texans for life, and Cowboys fans forever. (They are God's favorite football team, mind you. That's why there's a hole in the top of their stadium—so God can look down and watch His favorite team play.)

We now live in one of the forty-nine lesser states. But we never lost touch with our loved ones back home. One of them was a family friend named Rick Blinn. He and our dad had become close friends as they ministered together out in front of abortion clinics in Dallas.

We joked that Rick was far more pro-life than Dad—he had thirteen kids to Dad's five. He always said that he had four girls and nine boys, just to make it even. He sent us a picture once, of all the cereal boxes their family went through each morning to feed that many kids. Wow. It made us want to invest in Kellogg's and General Mills.

Rick worked as a general manager at a nationwide uniform manufacturer. After fourteen years of service, he was fired due to his pro-life activism. As a result, he got into the dry-cleaning business. Our sister, Tracy, worked for him. But money was hard to come by in that space, so he got out of that business.

While finances were in short supply for Rick and his family at that time, their faith—and faithfulness—was abundant.

They were some of the most authentic people we've ever met, ministering to young mothers and pregnant teenagers at abortion clinics all over Dallas. And any time our dad held a pro-life event, we always knew that if nobody else showed up, the Blinn family would be there.

Rick trained his kids to stand for life. But he didn't just teach them to defend the defenseless; he also taught them to help the helpless. He and his wife, Joan, adopted an orphan from Korea who had microcephaly, cerebral palsy, and profound retardation. He was an infant when they got him. The little guy was non-ambulatory, nonverbal, and incontinent, and would be for the rest of his life. When he arrived from Korea, he was having no less than 100 seizures a day. Due to his severe health issues, they had no idea how long his life on earth might be, but they committed to loving him through every single one of those days.

They named him Sam, but he always went by "Sam the Man." He would never utter a word or take a step or hug a neck, but the Blinn family took him in and treated him as one of their own. They fed him, bathed him, changed his diaper, and turned his wheelchair into the coolest ride you'd ever see. Rick and Joan knew this would be Sam's way of life when they adopted him, but they did it anyway because their hearts went out to this helpless boy who had no family of his own.

They had been warned that Sam would most likely not live past the age of fifteen. But thanks to the tender love and care of the Blinn family, he made it all the way to thirty-three.

We had grown up knowing of Rick's faithfulness and heart to help those who couldn't help themselves. So when he called one day in 2006 and asked to meet with us, we agreed wholeheartedly.

THE CONVERSATION AT STARBUCKS

By that time, we had built our little niche business into quite a powerhouse. We were selling more foreclosed houses than anyone in North Carolina, but we had pretty much capped out in the Charlotte market. If we wanted to sell more houses, we'd have to expand into other areas. But we had no idea how to do that.

One of our biggest clients was a bank in Dallas, so each year we'd fly to Big D to meet with the team there. Rick had gotten his real estate license earlier that year, so when Dad told him what we were doing and that we'd be in town, he asked if he could meet with us.

We're not the "let's meet at Starbucks" types. We'd prefer to meet at a gym and talk business after we've suffered through a workout. But Rick has gray hair and takes caffeine intravenously, so we went easy on the guy and reluctantly agreed to do the Starbucks thing.

"Guys, I gotta tell ya," Rick said as he sipped his straight black coffee, "we're struggling financially. I had to close the laundromat, then I took a few sales jobs, but none of them panned out. I got my real estate license hoping things would turn around. But it's just not happening, and I don't know what to do."

Everything inside of us wanted to jot him a check right then and there. He and his family, as faithful pro-life missionaries, were well worthy of financial support. But something was stirring in our hearts, like the catalyst of an idea that could help Rick not just one time, but for a long time.

Rick didn't need money. He needed an opportunity.

A few months earlier, we'd had a conversation with a client who said she wished she could clone us in Detroit because she needed more good agents in that area. In typical entrepreneur style, our first thought had been, *How can we make that happen?* But up to that point we hadn't done anything with it.

Yet the more Rick talked, the more our hearts began to burn. Almost in unison (which happens more than we'd like to admit), we said, "What if we could replicate what we're doing in Charlotte here in Dallas? Then you could be our agent here?"

"I would absolutely love that," Rick said without hesitation. "I need to do something, and fast."

Walking out of the Starbucks that day, we felt like we had when we got that phone call from Bill Spooner at the beginning of our business (back in Chapter Four). Our hearts were pounding as our brains were flooded with ideas on how we could grow and expand our little business into Dallas and ultimately markets across the nation. God had given us a new opportunity, and we were going to run after it with everything we had.

We sat in our rental car as Rick pulled off in his old dilapidated suburban. "We can do this," David said. "We can change the financial situation for the Blinn family if we figure this thing out."

This was the genesis of our idea to franchise our business. A phone call from a client who wished we could be cloned, followed by the desperate plea of a faithful father of fourteen was God's way of moving us in the direction He wanted us to go.

And move we did—fast! We divided and conquered. David took over the day-to-day business operations while I (Jason) ran full steam ahead on franchising our company. With Rick as our target franchisee, we racked our brains on how to set him up for success.

SETTING IT UP RIGHT

By God's grace, we figured it out. Just as we were able to complete a week's worth of tasks in a few hours for Bill Spooner, we were able to complete a year's worth of tasks in a few months for Rick Blinn. We focused on replicating our business and giving Rick an opportunity to crush it in the foreclosure space just as we were doing.

Fortunately, by then we had already systematized our business to a point where we could replicate it easily. (We'll share the specifics of how we did it in Part 2 of this book.) The most important thing for us at that point was *setting Rick up for success*. We knew that if we could do it for him, then we could certainly do it for others.

We give this advice to aspiring entrepreneurs: "Before you start any business, you need to have a clear picture in your mind of who you're going to serve."

- What does your ideal customer look like, dress like, act like, and spend like?
- Who are they and what makes them tick?
- What are their needs and goals?

Once you have that person in mind, they become your avatar; everything you do in your business is for them and them alone. Anyone who doesn't fit your avatar description is not your customer.

Rick was our avatar:

- A middle-aged person with a family
- Entrepreneurial-minded, but hadn't made a big break and needed an opportunity
- Never made much money, but had a blue-collar mindset (not afraid to get his hands dirty)
- A giver

That last part was important to us. We didn't want to help people make money who weren't givers by nature. (Rick had set the bar high for this one.) We wanted to help him make tons of money because we knew he would do good things with that money.

One of the first questions for us, aside from how we were going to structure things, was how much to charge. Because Rick was our avatar, we chose to forego the typical high-cost franchise fee and percentage-based royalty in exchange for an extremely low-cost, up-front fee with a per-transaction royalty. Even though we had been advised by friends and franchise consultants to charge much more, we wanted to do things differently.

A low barrier of entry would allow our franchisees to make the lion's share of the money. We had seen too many franchisors charge all sorts of fees and percentages, making it so that the franchisee could barely scrape by. We didn't want to do that, so we designed our money model for volume. If our franchisees sold a lot of property, then we made a lot of money. But if they didn't, then we wouldn't.

And to make things even better for them, we chose not to charge a monthly minimum like many other franchises did. If our franchisees weren't sellin' … they weren't payin'.

All of this was done because Rick Blinn was our avatar.

TURNING THE TABLES

After all the legal documents were drafted, the manuals written, and the branding trademarked, we gave Rick a call.

"You ready to do this?" we asked.

"What took you so long?" he replied. "I was ready the day we walked out of Starbucks!"

"Good," we replied. "You're our guinea pig, so we're going to gift this franchise to you. No up-front fee. You just pay the royalties."

It was silent on the other end for a moment. "I hate you guys," he finally said. "And I love you at the same time! Thank you. Joan and I really appreciate it. I promise you won't be disappointed."

A few days later, Rick flew into Charlotte. We spent several days training him on everything it took to manage and sell a bank-owned property. We built our system around two things: *speed and scale.* Rick learned that if he wanted to be successful in this business, he had to jump through both those hoops for banks.

"Move Fast, Manage Well" was our motto.

Before Rick returned to Dallas, we prayed together and dedicated his business to God, just as we had done for our own. We asked God to open doors miraculously and to endear our clients' hearts toward Rick in the same way we had experienced.

Then we got to work. We reached out to every bank we had dealings with and told them we had opened a new location in Dallas and were ready to start taking properties there. We assured them that they could expect the same level of service there as they got from us in North Carolina.

Properties started slowly trickling in. A few months went by, during which Rick proved he was up to the task ... and then the floodgates opened. One year later, Rick called.

"Boys, this is amazing!" he said. "I made more money last year than I made in the previous three years combined! Thank you so much for giving me the opportunity to provide for my family like this."

"We didn't do it for you," we replied. "We did it for Joan!"

"Good!" he said. "Because Joan wants to get her real estate license now!"

We hung up the phone with a sense of satisfaction we hadn't felt before. We thought back to that conversation in Starbucks and the choice we had to make: to give Rick money or give him an opportunity. We had chosen the latter and discovered something beautiful—the more money Rick made, the more money we made.

You've certainly heard the statement, "Give a man a fish and you'll feed him for a day. Teach a man to fish and you'll feed him for a lifetime." But entrepreneurs go one step further: We sell him a fishing pole![8] And we couldn't wait to make more poles.

Our little idea had worked. Realizing that the Blinns' financial situation was radically changed for the better because of the idea God gave us was overwhelmingly fulfilling. And slightly addicting, to be honest. We couldn't wait to announce it to the world.

But then God told us something that stopped us in our tracks.

---

[8] Original thought attributed to Peng Joon.

CHAPTER SEVEN

UNCONVENTIONAL

After witnessing Rick's success, we knew we could easily grow this thing. Our system was fully locked in and ready for scale. All we needed to do now was nail our marketing, begin advertising, and watch the sales skyrocket.

That's when God dropped an unconventional strategy into our heads: *Don't market this company. No advertising; let it grow organically.* Not that God was against marketing (we have since done it extensively in all our other businesses) but for this particular one, we felt God leading us down another path: to depend on prayer alone to build our first company.

That was a tough pill to swallow. It flew in the face of every business idea in the known world. But along with God's prompting, He gave us the power to obey. We thought of George Müller ... again. Only this time, we had the same marching orders he had—*build your business by relying on God alone and watch Him work!*

This is not to say marketing isn't pivotal to business. Quite the contrary. You can't scale a business without it. We've run several successful businesses that utilize marketing AND we trust God with those companies. But more important than marketing is hearing the voice of God and following that voice when He tells you to do something ... even if that something doesn't make sense.

When that happens, abandon your plan for His plan and enjoy the ride.

We didn't understand it then. But looking back, we can see why relying solely on prayer was the route God wanted us to go. It gave us a testimony of God's awesome power when partnering with Him.

Obeying the Lord when it didn't make sense gave us a God story about His faithfulness in our business. And having a testimony like this would help us continue to depend on Him through many difficult situations in the future.

But this decision to lean fully on God through prayer wasn't just for us ...

We believe it was for *you* as well.

Our story shows that you can trust God with your business. We believe that testimonies of God's enduring faithfulness showcase the supernatural power He can bring into any situation *if you let Him take the lead.*

Ultimately, building our franchise on prayer alone would allow God to get all the credit—and that, of course, is where the credit belongs. If we went the traditional route, our business would be just like any other success story—we went from rags to riches because *we* had an idea, *we* worked hard, *we* targeted the right people, and *we* had a few strokes of good luck along the way. People would be impressed with *us*! Yeah ... no.

It wasn't about us, and if we went the way God told us to go, people would be much more impressed with *Him*.

This isn't to say it was all smooth sailing. (For a while, those sails didn't seem to be getting even a puff of air.) We had serious doubts along the way. We weren't all "gung-ho" about this approach. Even after we started selling franchises, doubts remained. But we soon learned that when the doubts came, we had to choose to see things *spiritually* rather than *strategically*.

We had to keep our eyes on God and trust Him.

Strategy is important—extremely important—but if you want to make an impact for God through business, it's never meant to lead.

So, when God told us to grow our franchise without any marketing, we remembered the word He had given us a few years back in Keystone: *Focus on My thing and I'll focus on your thing*. Our faith back then intersected with God's faithfulness and became a testimony we held onto to pull us through a trial of faith. Only this time, the situation was different—at least, that's what we told ourselves. The conversation in our heads went something like this:

God, we know You came through for us in Keystone, and with Gramma giving us that money, and lots of other times in the past. But this time is different. We can't sell franchises if we don't do any marketing and advertising. Everyone knows that. Don't You? If we're going to scale this business, then we have no other choice.

Typically, this is the time God gets quiet. Funny how that works. We've discovered that when God speaks clearly to you, if you don't obey right away, He might not speak again. At least, not on that specific subject.

Thankfully, we finally decided to follow His instructions all the way. And the moment we surrendered to His plan, the phone started to ring.

Our first franchisee after Rick was a pastor in Pennsylvania who decided to get a real estate license to help offset his low salary. He had a mutual friend who told him that we worked with banks and had franchised into a second location. So he called out of the blue to see if he could open one in his city.

"Yeah, we'll let you open a location," we said. "But we ain't gonna sell it to you. You're a pastor, for crying out loud. Just open it and we'll deal with the money later."

> *Note: We saw those first two locations—in Texas and Pennsylvania—as our "firstfruits." In farming, firstfruits are the first agricultural produce of a season. In business, they're the initial results of your endeavor.*

> *All throughout the Bible, God talks about giving your tithes (10 percent off the top), offerings (spontaneous gifts of any amount), and firstfruits (100 percent of the first yield) from the money you make. He commands this because money represents security, and if you're willing to give Him your money, then it shows that you trust Him.*

> *We've always tithed on the net profit of our businesses each month and given offerings as God directs. But when we open a new business, oftentimes we'll donate all the profit from our first sale. In this way, we're honoring God as our business partner … He always gets the first cut.*

A few days after we opened our second location, we got a call from another friend of a friend who had a friend who heard of a guy who knew someone who met us one time at a high school football game … *you get the picture.* Calls like that quickly became the norm. We opened a third location, then a fourth, then a fifth. The phone never stopped ringing for three straight years until we reached our hundredth office in our thirty-fifth state, at which point we turned the faucet off and stopped selling franchises altogether.

All of this was done *without any marketing or advertising* whatsoever. Zero. Zilch. Nada. God told us to do it His way, we did, and He blessed it.

Like we said in the last chapter, partnering with God in your business is a smart decision. And when He asks you to do crazy things that don't make sense, *just do them!* Not only will you have cool stories to tell, but those tales will be full-on *God* stories that show people what an amazing business partner you have.

As business owners—and as individuals—our main responsibility is to bring God glory in all we do. This means we are to "put Him on display."[9] Just as you take a prized trophy and prominently display it for all to see, we are to do the same with God in our lives and businesses. We do this in the same way Jesus did when He walked the earth: "I have brought You glory on earth by *completing the work* you called Me to do" (John 17:5, emphasis added).

When you do good work, you put God on display for all to see. When you bring Him into the decision-making process of your business and walk in obedience to what He tells you to do—no matter how unconventional it may be—you make Him look good. And, as a faith-filled entrepreneur, there's no greater work you can do.

---

[9] Tony Evans, *The Kingdom Agenda* (Lifeway, 2013).

CHAPTER EIGHT

FULL TIME MINISTRY

Following God's lead, our franchise exploded. And each year our franchisees would fly in for our annual conference where we'd train them in kingdom business, eat good BBQ, and hit group workouts where some—not all—even threw up (true story). At one of these conferences, God spoke something to us that changed our lives forever.

In the introduction of this book, we shared about one of these conferences when we stood in front of our franchisees with our notes and an open Bible. I (Jason) talked about how the true definition of profit is not the surplus you have in your bank account at the end of the month—it's anything that leads to life. About halfway through my talk I heard God speak to me. I was a little caught off guard because I don't typically hear voices in my head (that's David's thing). But that morning I felt like I heard God whisper a question in my spirit.

"Who told you that you weren't in full-time ministry?"

That question may sound odd to you, but for me it rocked me to my core. It affected David the same way when I told him about it later that day.

You see, ever since we started our business we struggled with guilt for not going into "full-time ministry."

We had no idea that our entire paradigm of *ministry* was off. We even started thinking that maybe our role was to make money so we could fund ministries, but that paradigm was just as broken.

What we didn't realize then, but we know now, is that we were in ministry the whole time. We learned that where we're placed and how we're paid doesn't determine the minister. It's about God's presence in our lives and our passion to glorify Him through our work that makes us full-time ministers right where we are. It doesn't matter what we did for a living—ministry is about desire more than your duty. We had a desire to glorify God in our work and that's what made us ministers.

This is a breakthrough paradigm shift Satan doesn't want you to have. He knows that how you see yourself determines how you behave yourself. So if you see yourself as just an insurance agent, or banker, or contractor, or teacher, then that's how you'll behave. You won't act like the minister God made you to be.

Business is all about serving people. When you do it with a heart to please God you've now turned your business into a ministry. It's more than just *Business AS Mission*, it's *Business IS Mission*. You will see your business not just having *instrumental* value where you can use it to give money, but you will see it having *intrinsic* value where you can use it to do ministry.[10]

God asked Adam a similar question after he sinned in the Garden and hid himself because he realized, for the first time, he was naked. God asked him, "Who told you that you were naked?" (Genesis 3:11) God had to deal with the liar in Adam's ear before He could set him straight.

We had been lied to for the first six years of our business. We believed that the only ministers were the people who stood on stage and spoke and operated through a non-profit model, and that the only missionaries were the ones who went overseas and raised financial support. But these were lies Satan wanted

---

[10] Jeff Van Duzer, Why Business Matters to God

us to believe because he knew that if we saw our true identity as ministers on mission to represent God's kingdom to earth then he'd have a fight on his hands.

Billy Graham once said, "I believe the next great move of God will be among believers in the marketplace." We believe this too, and it starts when Christians in the workplace recognize their identities as ministers and their calling as missionaries.

God's question that day changed the trajectory of our lives. We no longer thought about getting out of business so we could enter into ministry. We thought about opening more businesses so we could do more ministry. Nothing in our circumstances had changed, but everything was different.

PARADIGM SHIFT

It reminded us of a story we read about a businessman in New York City. He was on the subway peacefully riding to church one Sunday morning. He and other passengers sat quietly reading the newspaper. Then a dad with three small kids entered the subway car. The moment they stepped in, the kids started yelling, throwing things, and running around the car—upsetting the once-peaceful atmosphere.

The dad sat there with his eyes closed, oblivious to the whole thing.

Clearly agitated, the businessman looked over at the dad and said, "Sir, your children are disturbing people. I wonder if you couldn't control them a little more?"

The dad looked up as if he were surprised at his kids' behavior. "Oh, you're right," he said softly. "I guess I should do something about it. We just came from the hospital where their mother died about an hour ago. I don't know what to do, and I guess they don't know how to handle it either."[11]

At that moment, everything changed. This flustered businessman who saw these kids as obnoxious and the dad as oblivious now viewed them through a lens of compassion rather than frustration. As a result, he was no longer angry, but broken over their situation. He didn't need a how-to list or a step-by-step process on how to help a hurting person. The compassion in his heart propelled him to act. He instinctively knew what to do because he saw the situation differently.

"Oh Sir" the businessman responded. " I'm so sorry! What can I do to help?"

Although nothing in the situation had changed, everything was different once he knew the truth.

The foundation of all good business is first knowing the truth of who you are. Our goal is not to simply give you another how-to book on the practical things you can do to build a business. While books like that are helpful—and we've read many of them—our focus is to give you a new lens through which you can view yourself and your business.

How you *see* determines how you *act*. When perception changes, behavior changes. The single best thing we've ever done in our business is change the way we *view* it.

We've seen firsthand the power of this shift in perspective. If we can get an entrepreneur to *see* differently, his behavior will change naturally. And when this happens, buckle up and get ready for the ride because it's going to be a wild one.

---

[11] Recounted in Stephen Covey's book *The Seven Habits of Highly Effective People*.

YOUR TRUE IDENTITY

When we coach entrepreneurs we always take them through the process in this order - paradigms, principles, practicals. Building your business on foundational principles is key, but all good principles are first derived from a proper paradigm.

God took the scales off our eyes that morning and showed us three paradigm-shifting truths that we now teach Christian entrepreneurs all over the world:

- You're a minister right where you are.
- You're on mission to bring God glory.
- Your work is worship.

If you don't get anything else out of this book other than these three truths, we will have accomplished our goal. When you know these truths and live them every day in your job or at your business, watch how God will show up and bless your socks off. You may not be blessed with financial profit, but you will certainly be blessed with spiritual peace. Best of all, you will become the person God created you to be—someone who will not gain the world and forfeit his soul.

From our paradigm-shifting moment forward everything changed for us. Our daily tasks turned into assignments from God. The people we worked with became a flock to be shepherded. Those we worked for turned into a mission field to be harvested. We no longer operated out of guilt for *not going into* ministry, but out of gratitude for *being in* ministry. Our sense of failure was replaced with fulfillment as we realized we were right where God wanted us using the talents He had given us to be good at that in which He called us.

As a result of our newfound identities as ministers in the marketplace, we pressed the gas on our entrepreneurial drives and let them fly. Soon, we found ourselves atop a family of companies—both for profit and nonprofit—across the nation and around the globe.

CHAPTER NINE

FAILING FORWARD

As our business grew, so did our income. We never expected it, nor was it something we sought, but in short order we went from making less than $40,000 combined in that first year of business to raking in several million. God had opened the floodgates.

But it wasn't easy to run a business that grew so big so fast, especially considering we had young families that also were growing rapidly. It seemed like every other year, one or the other of us was welcoming a new baby into the household. So we had to figure out how to get our business to run itself, and fast! We wanted to *own* it, not have it own us.

By God's grace, in the same way He brought success, He also directed us how to manage that success so that it didn't rob us of time with our families. Two years into franchising, by the time we reached our fiftieth location, we had fully removed ourselves from the business so that it could run without us. At the same time, we were able to remove ourselves from the company payroll. Our passive income from the investments we made exceeded our living expenses. By our thirty-third birthday in 2008, we were 100% financially free and out of the rat race.

This was a breakthrough we had worked and prayed for.

We knew full well that retirement was not an option. Our dad always taught us that the Bible doesn't endorse retirement—it endorses *re-tire*ment, where you put on new tires and keep moving forward. So that's what we did.

We shifted our focus from one business in the real estate industry to building several businesses in other industries, both for-profit and nonprofit. Our experience gave us the intellectual capital to do it, and our passive income gave us the time in our day to make it happen.

By the time HGTV came knocking on our door in 2013, we had grown from Benham Real Estate Group to Benham Companies, with businesses ranging from automotive marketing and software engineering to tax planning and commercial development. At the same time, we organized several nonprofit ventures and initiatives—from pro-life advocacy and Christian campgrounds to citywide outreach and global missions.[12]

But before you think that everything we touch turns to gold, you need to know we've made plenty of bone-headed mistakes along the way. We've learned the hard way on several occasions—a few we'd like to forget.

Like SillyBandz. Do you remember those little rubber things kids went crazy over? Geez. How stupid were we? We jumped into that business with a buddy of ours from church. We quickly learned that just because you're reading the same book doesn't mean you're on the same page.

Our subject-matter expert (SME) loved the Lord and was entrepreneurial, just like us, but he was in a *wants*-based business dealing B-to-C, which certainly was not our wheelhouse. We knew this about ourselves, yet we did it anyway because we were sure we could make a profit.

Lesson: Doing something outside our lane in order to make a profit was not a good idea.

---

[12] See Appendix A to learn more about our *Misioneering* effort overseas.

We also failed epically in the vending-machine space. Another buddy of ours owned a vending business that we thought we could expand all over the country. Our idea was to buy a bunch of machines and then finance them back to people, giving folks a low barrier of entry to own a business of their own.

Our idea was bigger than our buddy's capacity, but we were attached to it and went with it anyway. Epic failure.

Lesson: When you don't have someone who can implement your idea, it's best to let it go.

Those little fiascos cost us more money than we made, but they taught us some valuable lessons. For instance, once you realize the business is going to fail, make sure it fails fast. If you see it going down, jump out of it faster than you got into it. Don't let your heart make the decision, otherwise you'll stay too long. Reduce it to a simple number (the amount of money you're going to lose), remove the emotion, and bail.

Another lesson we learned through those experiences involves knowing *when* to jump into a venture in the first place. We learned that, before we got into a new business, three things had to be present:

- Potential. It had to be something that could make good money (inside our competency or the competency of an SME).
- Opportunity. It had to give us the opportunity to be absentee owners (with a good SME).
- The Smile of God. The Lord needed to stamp His approval on our involvement.

The first two points are what most entrepreneurs need before they jump into a new venture. But it's the third one that makes all the difference. If you want to be someone who not only earns an income but also makes an impact, then you need to wait for the smile of God before you move forward.

Waiting is hard for an entrepreneur. But it's during that time, as you continue to pray and think, that God will speak to your spirit about what you should do.

We learned this (the hard way) on a much larger scale when we decided to build a new office for our rapidly growing company. This was back in early 2008, just months before the real estate market crashed. We fell in love with a piece of land close to our houses (we live down the street from each other), yet the price was high, and it would require a huge retaining wall—something that was certainly not cheap. Although half the property was in a wetland, the location was epic. The more we prayed about it the more we felt like it was the place for us.

The only problem was that God had convicted us to no longer use debt in our business; that if He wanted us to buy something, He'd provide the cash. But because we're ambitious entrepreneurs who know how to make things happen, we rationalized that building a new office didn't count.

Our ambition jumped into the driver's seat and stepped on the gas (not wise). We obtained a $1.3 million loan and started construction, giving the job to the lowest bidder (also not wise). To make the place even bigger, we added more than $500,000 of our own cash to the project.

A year later, and only two months after we'd moved in, the forty-foot retaining wall at the back of our building collapsed. It sounded like an earthquake; the entire building shook. Every person in the place ran outside, afraid the whole building was going to go down.

Fortunately, there was enough flat land underneath the building that it didn't fall into the wetlands below. But the back corner was literally suspended in mid-air above a forty-foot sheer cliff of dirt. In the months that followed, we spent over $1 million to rebuild that sucker. The first night alone, we had to spend nearly $100,000 just to secure the building.

We tell the full story in our book *Whatever the Cost*. But the main thing we learned from that debacle is that God's "yes" and God's "go" are two different things. They are typically separated by a period of waiting, where God makes you into the person who can handle what He said yes to.

God said "yes" to us buying that land. But He hadn't given us the green light to move forward just yet. Because we chose to proceed in our own timing by using a massive amount of debt, we lost money ... lots of it. If we would have simply waited one year—with the real estate crash that took place—we could have bought the land *and* built the building with cash.

We learned from that boneheaded mistake that when God wants you to move forward on something, the doors will open automatically. You won't have to kick them open; you won't have to engage all your ambition to *make* it happen.

The fact that we had to do some "creative financing" to buy the land and build the building should've been our cue to wait. The minute we felt ourselves striving to make something happen, we should have paused and waited for God to move.

This doesn't mean using debt in business is wrong. You should run with the convictions God gives you for your particular business approach. But we pushed too hard, too fast. And because we refused to wait, we fell out of step with God's best for our business.

Waiting involves faith, and faith is *living without scheming*.[13] Yet our ambition didn't want to wait. So we let it jump out of the passenger's seat into the driver's seat and take over. As a result, we paid dearly.

---

[13] Warren Wiersbe, *BE Commentaries* (David C. Cook, 2007).

We simply want to assure you that when we talk about our businesses and all the success we've experienced, you need to know it's not void of some absolutely idiotic moves on our part. By God's grace, though, our successes have outpaced our failures.

SYSTEM OF SUCCESS

After the wall debacle, we were finally able to settle comfortably into a business-building cycle that looked something like this:

- Start a business.
- Build it to a point where it could run itself (by developing systems).
- Position an SME for success (by letting them take ownership, offering strategic leadership, and helping build a team).
- Manage the money until the business is self-sustaining.
- Invest the active income from the business into passive income assets (such as real estate and other small businesses).
- Move on to the next new venture.

As we moved from one business to the next, we realized that we had unknowingly *created a system of success that applied to all industries.* If we applied certain principles in a particular order, we could build a solid organization regardless of the vertical. Whether nonprofit or for-profit, our system worked.

We dubbed this system *Expert Ownership* because it shows you how to own your business (or organization) without it owning you, so you can focus on impact over income. That's what true Expert Owners do. They don't build companies that rob them of the things that matter most in life—relationships with the people they love. They create businesses that give them the ability to do great things and to bless others, while maintaining the freedom to be with their families, especially during their kids' formative years.

A true Expert Owner knows how to serve God, thrive in business, and live a life of impact—all at the same time.

So, having developed this system and seen it launch successful businesses time and again, we've dedicated the rest of our lives to helping people like you become Expert Owners. Teaching this system is one of the ways we've *re-tired* and why we're so jazzed about the next fifty years of our lives (our grandma is ninety-two, so we're hoping we have her genes!).

Here's the deal: We firmly believe that God is raising up an army of entrepreneurs who can and will achieve breakthroughs in business so they can do awesome things in the world, so they can start nonprofits that change lives and shape culture, or other for-profits that generate wealth and provide jobs. They don't fear failure. And when they do fail, they fail forward: They get up, dust themselves off, and jump back into the game.

God is calling all of us to a higher playing field in business. And the steps we're about to give you will help you get there.

PART TWO

The Expert Ownership
Twelve-Step System

EXPERT OWNERSHIP

12 STEP PROCESS

SeeYaPreneur

↗ 12. Money

/ 11. Leadership

/ 10. Team Building

/ 09. Systems

/ 08. Value Delivery

/ 07. Sales

/ 06. Marketing

/ 05. Value Creation

/ 04. Branding

/ 03. Ideation

/ 02. Core Four

/ 01. Identity

We broke our Expert Ownership system into twelve steps because Jesus had twelve disciples. Not really, but it sounds cool, right? *(David: Jason isn't that spiritual.)* In reality, as we look back on how we started, scaled, and sold businesses in the past, these twelve steps are the natural progression we took each time.

We've divided the system into three key modules:

1. Mindset
2. Movement
3. Momentum

Get the right *mindset* about your business, start *moving* in the right direction, then let your *momentum* take over. In time, you'll be able to remove yourself from the business altogether.

Each module contains four steps. Here's a quick overview:

MODULE 1:
MINDSET—How You Think About Your Business

In this module, we guide you on how to get inside your head and pull out the nuggets of gold that will help you achieve your dreams in business. It includes these four steps:

- *Identity*—understand who you are and what you have to offer the world.
- *Core Four*—define your mission, vision, values, and principles that will guide you.
- *Ideation*—generate ideas that will make money and fall within your sweet spot.
- *Brand*—define the unique way you will solve your customers' problems.

MODULE 2:
MOVEMENT—How to Get Your Business Moving in the Right Direction

The second module takes you from idea to reality so you can build a legitimate business around your dream. Movement includes these four steps:

- *Value Creation*—define your value proposition and the plan to make it happen.
- *Marketing*—learn how to generate prospects.
- *Sales*—turn your prospects into purchasers.
- *Value Delivery*—turn your purchasers into promoters.

MODULE 3:
MOMENTUM—How to Scale Your Business to the Next Level

This final module shows you how to scale your business to the masses while removing yourself from the day-to-day operations. This is the module where we show you how to achieve "SeeYaPreneur status." It includes these four steps:

- *Systems*—develop systems so you can work *on* the business and not *in* it.
- *Team Building*—attract people who can run the system you've developed.
- *Leadership*—learn the ability to create healthy appetites in those you lead.
- *Money*—convert your cash into cash flow and become a SeeYaPreneur for life.

As we said at the beginning, these steps will help you no matter where you are in your business journey. You might need help starting a business, or you'd like ideas on how to scale the one you already have, or you want some advice on how to motivate your team … or maybe you just want some good old-fashioned ideas on what to do with your money.

Regardless of your particular circumstances, what we'll share in the following pages will help you. When we're done, you will have the tools you need to become an Expert Owner who can serve God, thrive in business, and live the life of impact you've always dreamed about.

STEP ONE

IDENTITY

SeeYaPreneur

↗ 12. Money

/ 11. Leadership

/ 10. Team Building

/ 09. Systems

/ 08. Value Delivery

/ 07. Sales

/ 06. Marketing

/ 05. Value Creation

/ 04. Branding

/ 03. Ideation

/ 02. Core Four

/ **01. Identity**

CHAPTER TEN

IDENTITY:
KNOW WHO YOU ARE

The first step in our Expert Ownership system is all about identity. Why? Because all good business is born out of *who you are* as a person. Entrepreneurs, at their core, are "*you*preneurs." In other words, your business is a reflection of yourself. That's why we start by discussing the type of person you are at work and the *type of person you need to be* if you want to succeed in business.

We discussed in chapter eight the identity you received the day you surrendered your heart to the Lord. You became a minister on mission and your work became your primary form of worship. But what we want to talk about in this chapter is how your identity plays itself out practically in the workplace. To do that, we look to the game of baseball.

Throughout our time as business owners, we've discovered that business and baseball have a lot of similarities. (Admittedly, we're a little better at business than we were on the ballfield.) Both have taught us to deal with curveballs. (*Jason: something David always struggled with!*) So, we'll be using the game as an analogy throughout these remaining chapters.

The first and most important lesson we learned is this: in order to succeed in baseball, you have to move *backward* before moving *forward*.

If you want to throw a ball to home plate, you don't just grab the ball and throw your hand toward the plate with the ball. You have to swing your arm backward in order to gain momentum to throw it forward.

The same is true with hitting. You don't just take the bat and launch forward—you'll have zero momentum to generate any power. You have to shift backward in order to build momentum to launch forward. *And* you have to keep your eye on the ball—otherwise you'll end up whiffing! *(David: Jason did that a lot—it was sad to watch.)*

The same is true in business. When aspiring or existing entrepreneurs come to us with an idea of *what* they want to do, we immediately tell them to pause, take a few steps back, and first ask themselves the *who* and *why* questions.

1. W*ho* am I?

2. *Why* do I want to be in business?

It's easy to talk about *what* you want to do. But if you want your business dream to transform into a reality, the two things you have to be crystal clear on are *who* you are and *why* you want to accomplish it. If you don't go back and answer these questions before moving forward, you may achieve *some* success, but not the kind you need to make a lasting impact ... and not the kind that brings you peace.

A few years into our first business, the two of us read a study referenced by the *Harvard Business Review* that listed the top characteristics of successful business leaders. Do you know what the #1 characteristic was?

Self-awareness.

We hadn't seen that coming. But it's true—knowing who you are and why you do what you do lies at the foundation of all truly significant endeavors. In this chapter, we're going to help you clarify *who* you are, and in the next we'll crystalize *why* you're in business. These next few chapters will help you take that shift back before moving forward, enabling you to generate the power you'll need to build a business that will last.

WHO ARE YOU?

We've discovered through the years that to be a successful business owner—one who experiences success in *all* areas of life, including faith, family, finances, fitness, and friendships—you need to know who you are in these five core areas:

1. Character

2. Work Ethic

3. Personality

4. Professional Ability

5. Emotional Intelligence

These five areas are ones we've seen directly connected to the success of our business, and it's these to which we pay close attention as we coach entrepreneurs and business leaders across the country.

So let's dive in.

CHARACTER

Character is doing what's right, *as God defines right*, even when nobody's watching.[14] The foundation of all good business is built upon character. When it comes to discovering what type

---

[14] Andy Stanley gave this definition in his sermon series titled *"Character Under Construction."* It is available for download from North Point Resources, https://store.northpoint.org/products/character-under-construction-audio-download.

of character you have in business, there are three key questions you need to ask:

- Am I a producer or a consumer?
- Am I a fountain or a drain?
- Am I a thermostat or a thermometer?

These questions are tough, because we have to be honest with ourselves in order to get to the root of the matter.

First, when it comes to being a producer, ask yourself, "Do I think more about what I can *get* or what I can *give*?" The difference between a giver and a getter is a matter of what motivates you.

A buddy of ours framed this perfectly at our Bible study. He's a young entrepreneur, and his business is taking off like a rocket. We asked him how he was doing it, and he said:

"When I worked in the financial services industry, I was taught to focus on *sales, sales, sales*. But when I started my own business, that mindset didn't feel right, so I flipped it around. My focus since day one has been to *serve, serve, serve*. I let the sales take care of themselves."[15]

Of course, the greatest example of someone motivated by selfless service is Jesus Christ. The night before He was betrayed, He took a towel and washed the feet of his employees (okay, they were disciples, but you get the idea). This set the stage for those men to make an impact so incredible we're still talking about it two thousand years later.

Now let's apply this concept of giving versus getting to your money. Being a producer by serving well means you *don't consume all the profit*. Instead, you *reinvest it* to help your business become even more productive. This is how you build

---

[15] This quote is from Keanu Trujillo with True Strategy.

a business with true sustainability of service that will be profitable regardless of the economy.

The second question you should ask is, "Am I a fountain or a drain?"

Do you bring life to others, or do you drain them?

When you go up to a water fountain and push the button, what comes out? Water, of course. And it refreshes you. Business is a context where your buttons get pushed *all the time*! And when they do, it's our responsibility as business leaders to make sure we're refreshing those who push our buttons.

The only way to do this is to be tapped into a pure source, just like a water fountain is tapped into the source of water. That pure source is the God who created you. When you tap into His power, you will become the life-giver He made you to be, even when it's hard.

Ask yourself, "Do the people I interact with on a daily basis, inside and outside of the business, feel refreshed by me, or drained by my presence? Does my life, with the words I say, the things I do, and the attitudes of my heart reveal that I'm a fountain ... or a drain?"

Lastly, when it comes to character, are you a thermostat or a thermometer? A thermometer *reflects* its environment, but a thermostat *transforms* it.

When the heat rises in a room, a thermometer goes right up with it, simply reflecting the rise in temperature. But a thermostat brings down the heat in a room with a cool breeze, creating a whole new level of comfort for everyone.

An Expert Owner transforms his or her atmosphere like a thermostat—they don't simply reflect it. People have needs, wants, demands … you name it. And *you* are the one who brings solutions, suggestions, peace, and provision—regardless of how emotionally hot or cold it may get around you.

Ask yourself, "Do I *reflect* the atmosphere or *transform* it? What kind of atmosphere am I creating? Is it an atmosphere that people want to be a part of? Are others drawn to it?"

So when it comes to building a business, it's important to reflect on these three core questions. But don't stop there! Adjust as you see fit. It might be a challenge, but making these changes is a vital part of shifting yourself into the right position to take a swing that will actually make contact.

The key is, by asking these simple questions—*Am I a producer or a consumer? Am I a fountain or a drain? Am I a thermostat or thermometer?*—you can discover the core of who you are.

Now, let's move on to the *way* you work.

WORK ETHIC

Achieving anything worthwhile, especially a successful business, takes hard work. It takes what we call the Tripod of Success:

1. Discipline

2. Diligence

3. Determination

Discipline is doing what you don't want to do to accomplish what you truly want.

Diligence is consistent movement in a positive direction, even when you can't see the results. It's the persistent application of discipline.

Determination is the burning desire to accomplish something worthwhile.

All great initiatives start with a burning desire. Your determination is what pushes you through the pain (think Rocky Balboa!). When you wrap discipline and diligence around a burning desire, nothing can stop you.

We saw this firsthand when we were fourteen years old. As eighth graders, we wanted to dunk a basketball, but we could barely touch the middle of the net. And that movie starring Wesley Snipes and Woody Harrelson, *White Men Can't Jump*, had just come out. We felt like we were doomed from the start. *(David: especially Jason. He jumped like he was wearing ankle weights.)*

But we *really* wanted to dunk. So, we created a little jumping workout and got up early every morning to hit it before we went to school. It was an absolute butt-kicker, yet slowly but surely, as we stuck with it, our leaping ability began to increase. By the time we were freshmen in high school, we were both slamming the ball. (We know, you're impressed.)

A decade later, when it came time to build a business, we remembered those early days and used the same three principles.

- **Determination.** We started with a burning desire to be financially free, which morphed into a passion to build businesses that had lasting impact around the world.
- **Discipline.** We did a lot of things we didn't want to do in order to make our dream a reality.
- **Diligence.** We never gave up our consistent effort to see it through.

Now, here we are writing a book on what the Lord enabled us to accomplish by standing on the Tripod of Success.

If you want to earn lasting wealth, the kind that can never be taken away from you, you need to build upon discipline, diligence, and determination. These three qualities will transform you into the kind of entrepreneur who can make an impact that will last a lifetime.

PERSONALITY

Now let's talk about your personality.

Even though we're twins, we have totally different personalities. *(Jason: David wants to be more like me.)* Early on in business, this was a rub; we'd find ourselves with overlapping responsibilities, which would proceed to knock-down, drag-out arguments.

So we ended up taking a couple of personality tests—Strengths Finder and the Myers Briggs 16 Personalities. And voila! Just like that, things began to fall into place in our minds and in our work. We discovered that taking these tests not only helped us get along better, but also illuminated the core strengths we needed to harness so that we could maximize our ability to succeed.

I (David) am more of an inspirer. Jason is more of an activator.

I am more people-driven. Jason is more process-driven.

Simply knowing these things about ourselves (and each other) helped us build our company. I took on more of the sales roles that used to frustrate Jason, while he took over the system development that drained me. The next thing we knew, we went one whole month without a single argument. (Our mom was really proud.)

Later in our business, we discovered the Enneagram and took that test as well. I (David) am an eight. I'm a challenger who wants to conquer the world (or so it says). Jason is a one. He's a moral perfectionist who wants to make the world a better place by reforming it from bad to good.

You don't need to have a business partner to take a personality test, but taking one—or several—will certainly be eye-opening. We encourage every business leader we consult to take them. You'll discover as you go that knowing your personality type will help you refine the *what* of your business much more easily.

We partnered with a company to build an Enneagram assessment of our own—you can take it at ExpertOwnership.com/Enneagram.

PROFESSIONAL ABILITY

When it comes to running your business, every entrepreneur naturally adopts one of three distinct personalities in the way they think about and operate within their business:

- Doer
- Developer
- Dreamer

If you're a *doer*, you thrive on getting your hands dirty, doing the technical details of the business. Doers are the people who know how to get it done. They thrive on being hands-on.

D*evelopers*, on the other hand, thrive on getting things done *through others*. They are managers by nature and love to get people moving in the same direction by operating through a system. Developers are implementers; they know how to take an idea and make it happen.

D*reamers* are your pure entrepreneurs. They come alive when there is a problem that needs a solution. A dreamer sees opportunities when others see obstacles, and the words "no" and "can't" are not in their vocabulary. A dreamer, however, cannot survive without a developer and a doer.[16]

Here's the key—all of us have a little bit of each type inside of us. But only one of them is our super-power. Both of us happen to be Dreamer types, so we had to specialize in attracting Doers and Developers who could take our ideas and make them a reality. In the beginning, before we knew about our particular strengths, we were both fully hands-on and did all the work in developing our rapidly growing employee base.

There's nothing wrong with running a business where you wear all three hats. Nearly everyone starting a business will need to do that for a time. But if you want any hope of moving from solopreneur to entrepreneur and eventually SeeYaPreneur, you need to try to operate as much as possible in Dreamer mode. Fortunately for us, as we grew, we figured out how to put ourselves in that position, which helped us expand into other businesses.

Michael Gerber, author of *The E-Myth Revisited,* says that most businesses are not started by entrepreneurs; they are started by technicians who had an entrepreneurial seizure.[17] This is also one of the reasons many small businesses fail in the first five years.

A business started by a Doer will keep him trapped *in* the business to where he has no time to work *on* it. He's too busy doing all the work, so he stays locked in solopreneur status without any chance of moving up the ladder. But to move from solopreneur to entrepreneur, he has to shift from a Doer into a Developer by building a system, and from a Developer into a Dreamer by hiring a team to run the system.

---

[16] Michael Gerber, in his book *The E-Myth Revisited: Why Most Small Businesses Don't Work and What To Do About It* (Harper Business, 2004),calls these the Technician, Manager, Entrepreneur.
[17] Ibid.

So how do you know which one you are?

Pay attention to your energy levels when you go about your daily tasks.

We both realized, early on, that doing the technical aspect of our business drained us so much that by the end of the day, we had no energy for anything else—even activities we'd typically love, like playing catch with the kids or shooting hoops in the backyard.

The same was true when it came to managing people. We thought we'd be great managers, but we quickly learned that dealing with employees every day sucked the life out of us.

It wasn't until we trained a few employees (Developers) to manage our people (Doers) that we found ourselves feeling energized every day to go to work. We were finally in a position to think creatively about moving the business forward because we were no longer trapped inside it, while our system gave us the ability to keep tabs on everything that was happening day-to-day.

This is the position we want you to be in—full Dreamer mode. You can still be a Doer and Developer if you *want* to, but when you unlock your inner Dreamer, you won't *have* to. And when you get to the chapter on ideation, we'll help you do just that.

EMOTIONAL INTELLIGENCE

The final component of discovering *who you are* is to understand your emotional intelligence.

If you haven't heard of this before, it's similar to your IQ (or your cognitive intelligence), which is how smart you are with *facts*. Your EQ (emotional quotient) is how good you are with *feelings*, and how well you manage your feelings in your relationships with others.

This stuff is super important. Successful people almost always have high emotional intelligence; it's just never been a *thing* before. Now, leaders around the world have come to recognize how important it is in business.

Emotional intelligence is the capacity to be aware of, control, and express your emotions, and to handle interpersonal relationships judiciously and empathetically.[18] Basically, if you're emotionally intelligent, it means you're *really* good with people. And as we said before, if you're good with people, you can crush it in business … because business is all about helping people.

According to research, people with a high EQ outperform those with a high IQ *70 percent of the time.* Roughly 90 percent of high performers at work are high in EQ. And people with high EQ make $29,000 more in salary on average than those with low EQ.[19]

These are some astounding statistics that convey just how vital it is that entrepreneurs understand and develop emotional intelligence. It's a crucial step backward to gain momentum forward.

I (Jason) did a lot of work in the field of emotions back when I earned my master's degree in counseling. My wife, Tori, is also a certified emotional intelligence coach. For this reason, David lets me take the lead on this topic (he could use a little emotional training himself!) (David: he's still bitter that I was better at basketball than him).

---

[18] Dictionary.com
[19] Travis Bradberry, *Emotional Intelligence 2.0* (TalentSmart, 2009).

Emotional intelligence consists of four key components—
self-awareness, self-management, social awareness, and
relationship management. The more you excel at each of
these, the more emotionally intelligent you are.

A **self-aware** person knows why they do what they do and
is aware of the emotions and tendencies that fuel their
actions.

A **self-managed** person is someone who can properly manage
their emotions and direct their behavior positively. They are
self-controlled.

A **socially aware** person is aware of the emotions of those
around them and is able to understand what's really going on
with them. They are empathetic.

The first three all lead to **relationship management**, where
emotionally intelligent people use their self- and social
awareness to successfully manage their interactions with
others.

But there's one more component of emotional intelligence
that my wife and I teach couples when we do marriage
seminars. It's the fifth component of EQ, and one that few
people talk about: *motivation*.

You can be an emotionally intelligent person and yet use
that high EQ to take advantage of others. In that case, your
motivation is selfish. But the path of the Expert Owner is
born out of a motivation to serve others and help them get
what *they* need, not to simply get what *you* want.

We can't say enough about how important emotional
intelligence is. There are entire books written on this topic
alone. When you're aware of your emotions and able to
control them, and you're aware of those around you and able
to manage your relationships with them, you're well on your

way to building a business that will serve people in a powerful way.[20]

KNOCK IT OUT OF THE PARK

So, you've already stepped up to the plate. The bat's in your hand. You just need to know exactly *who you are* before taking a swing. This healthy aspect of self-awareness will help give you the momentum you need to absolutely crush it in business.

Clarifying *who you are* is the first component of taking a step back before moving forward. In the next chapter, we'll look at the second component: getting your eye on the ball by clarifying *why* you want to be in business in the first place.

---

[20] You can take an emotional intelligence test at TalentSmart.com.

STEP TWO

CORE FOUR

_____

SeeYaPreneur

↗ 12. Money

/ 11. Leadership

/ 10. Team Building

/ 09. Systems

/ 08. Value Delivery

/ 07. Sales

/ 06. Marketing

/ 05. Value Creation

/ 04. Branding

/ 03. Ideation

/ **02. Core Four**

/ 01. Identity

CHAPTER ELEVEN

CORE FOUR:
ESTABLISH YOUR STANDARDS

I (David) still remember our first Little League baseball practice. We were five years old, and Dad took us out to the field. Jason had been crying because he didn't want to play, but I was thrilled at the chance. *(Jason: I didn't like competition when I was young, so cut me some slack!)*

The coach had us pick up bats to get ready to hit. I stepped up to the plate first and smacked the ball way over the outfielders' heads. But when Jason got up there, it was an entirely different story. The poor little dude couldn't sniff the ball. His head was flying back and forth—and the harder he tried, the worse it got.

The coach finally said, "Jason, why don't you try the other side of the plate."

Then he stepped across the plate into the other batter's box. The first pitch came, and ... "Whack!" Then again. "Whack!" It was borderline miraculous. *(Jason: There was nothing was miraculous about it—I just needed someone to put me on the other side of the plate so I could SEE the ball ... that's all).*

It turned out Jason was right-eye dominant and couldn't see the ball as a right-handed hitter. So, every time he took a swing, his bat was in the wrong place. But when he switched to a "lefty" pose, he could finally see it. From then on it was nothing but miracle after miracle!

We mentioned this earlier, but it begs repeating: When it

comes to hitting a baseball, you've got to shift back before you go forward. And you have to keep your eye on the ball. At that point, you can guide your bat to the proper place to make contact. It *sounds* easy, but executing it is a different story.

Translated into business terms, shifting back is all about knowing *who* you are. We talked about that in the previous chapter. Getting your eye on the ball is knowing *what* you're swinging at and *why* you're in the game in the first place. Even more, it's about guiding yourself to the right place to make contact.

Simply put, to be an Expert Owner, you need to know your vision, mission, values, and principles. Or the *CORE FOUR,* as we call them.

Vision is *what* you want to accomplish—it's what you're swinging at.

Mission is *why* you want to accomplish it—the reason you're in the game.

Values and principles become the guides to help you get there—and win the game.

- What do you want to accomplish in life?
- What about in your business?
- Why do you want to do it?
- What are the rules you're going to play by?

Answering these questions will help you further establish the foundation you need to build something great.

VISION & MISSION

Vision and mission were made to work together. That's why we rarely talk about one without the other. If you know what you want to do but don't know why you're doing it, then you'll burn out. If you know why you want to do something but have no clue what to do, you'll never get started. That's why you need to clearly define both your vision and mission up front.

Vision is like the lid on a jigsaw puzzle. When you open the box and dump all the pieces out, what's the first thing you do? You look at the picture on the lid. Imagine if you threw the lid away—how successful would you be at assembling the pieces?

Nothing happens if you don't have a clear picture of what you're building. This is why some marketing professionals define a company's vision as "who we are." Vision gives you a clear picture of who you are as a business.

Your vision guides you to put the right pieces in the right places. As Andy Stanley says, "The clearer the vision, the fewer the options, the easier the decision."[21]

This is the power of vision. But vision alone won't get you where you ultimately want to go. At least, not if you want to be an Expert Owner. It may lead to *success*, but lasting *significance* is only accomplished when you clearly know *why* you're doing it in the first place.

Knowing your *what* gives you the direction you need to go.

Knowing your *why* gives you the energy to do it.

This is where mission comes into play. While vision gives you direction, mission fuels your tank.

Imagine walking down the street and seeing three men, each mixing a bucket of concrete. You walk up to the first guy and ask, "What are you doing?"

"Mixing concrete," he says, wiping the sweat from his brow.

---

[21] Andy Stanley, *Visioneering* (Multnomah, 2005).

You ask the second guy, "What are *you* doing?"

"Pouring a foundation for a building," he says, looking behind him and pointing at the structure.

Then you ask the third guy, "What are *you* doing?"

He stops. Putting down his mixing tool, he says, "I'm building a children's hospital to help sick kids find health and wholeness."

Which one of these dudes do you think is going to persevere through the heat, the blisters, and the strain of mixing concrete day in and day out for months before seeing any success?

The third man, of course. He clearly knows his *what* (building a children's hospital) and his *why* (to help sick kids). He's got his eye locked in on the vision and mission for his work. And it gives him the ability *and* energy to keep his eye on the ball and knock his job out of the park. You'll especially see the power of a clearly defined vision and mission when it comes to teambuilding. But that's for a later chapter.

Here's the key:

We're talking about more than just establishing a vision and mission for your *business*. We're talking about creating them *personally* as well. So, when it comes to defining your vision and mission, you need to clearly define it in two ways:

- **Personal**—what you want to accomplish in life and why.
- **Professional**—what you want to accomplish with your business and why.

LET'S GET PERSONAL

Your business grows out of who you are and what you want in life. If you didn't have certain personal dreams and goals, you would never have ventured into the world of business in the first place.

When the two of us first got into business, our "why" was pretty simple—we just wanted to provide for our families. It wasn't super noble or anything, like building an orphanage, but it was definitely a legit reason to be in business.

But we had a feeling we needed to expand our purpose a bit more. In order to build something significant, we needed to ask ourselves exactly why we wanted to own a business and succeed with it. So, we spent some time thinking and praying, poring through our years of experience and everything we'd seen that had influenced us along the way.

We kept coming back to how our parents always told us we had the "gift of gab," and they knew God would use it one day to help others. As students, we used it to disrupt classes with well-timed jokes. As athletes, we used it to argue with umpires about bad calls. But as adults, we wanted to use it in a way to help others grow close to God. The only problem was, we had to work for a living, so we didn't get to use that gift very much.

So when we found ourselves jobless back in January of '03, we thought deeply on what we wanted to accomplish personally. That's when we started Benham Brothers Ministries, as we told you back in Chapter Four. But after God told us not to go that route and we found ourselves working in real estate, we settled on this personal vision and mission statement:

- We want to be financially free [our *what*] so we can minister to people through speaking and writing [our *why*].

Obviously, we were not able to do this at first. We still needed to work, and work hard, to make a living and support our families. But it became the goal that we obsessed over.

We wanted to be influencers—to help others through speaking and writing. We knew we had a gift to do this, but we didn't want to rely on getting paid to do it. Growing up poor sealed the deal on that one. We wanted to make money outside of speaking and writing, and when we read *Rich Dad, Poor Dad* by Robert Kyosaki, we realized there was a way to make it happen. (In our chapter on money, we'll dive deeper into this.)

The idea of becoming influencers who didn't have to depend on support from the people we influenced burned in our hearts. For us, that was an idea that had legs.

One of the questions that helped us drill this down was this: "What would we do if money wasn't an issue?" That's a great question for you as well. If you didn't have to think about money, what would you do with your time that would benefit others?

Influencing others through speaking and writing was our answer to that question.

LET'S DO BUSINESS

With our *personal* vision and mission firmly in place, we knew we needed to develop the same thing for our *business*.

The vision for our business was easy—to become the leading foreclosure brokers in the country. We knew that from the minute we received those first few bank-owned homes to sell.

But it was the mission we had to wrestle with. We wanted our *why* to be bigger than just freeing us up to speak and write.

That was great for us personally, but it would hardly attract others professionally.

So we started thinking about what energized us that was bigger than ourselves, a cause we could rally a team around.

When thinking about why we wanted to crush it in business, we thought back to our pro-life upbringing and how life-changing it was for us to see hurting moms receive support in their greatest moment of need. The more we thought about it, the more we realized how *ourbusiness* could help fund efforts like these, which would greatly impact our culture for good.

We knew that if our business succeeded, it could not only provide hope for families facing unplanned pregnancies but also be a part of bringing abortion to an end—to stand for life in the midst of a culture set on destroying it. That was something worth fighting for.

Armed with our why, we crafted a simple vision and mission statement for our business:

> "We will be the leading foreclosure brokers in the country [our *what*] so that we can breathe life into communities across the nation [our *why*]."[22]

We break this down further in our chapter on teambuilding. After all, the power of a clearly defined vision and mission for your business isn't just for your benefit; it's for those who work for you. It unites and mobilizes them around a common purpose and keeps them fired up to come to work!

Note: As you grow in business, you can break your

---

[22] Another way to look at your corporate vision and mission is this: vision is "who we are" and mission is "what we do." In our example, "who we are" is the leading foreclosure brokers in the country; "what we do" is breathe life into communities across the nation. We discuss this in detail in our course Expert Ownership: Mastering Marketing.

vision and mission into two separate statements. Many businesses have both a vision statement and a mission statement. But at the start, we like the simplicity of having one unifying statement.

Our *mission* gave us the energy to pursue our *vision*; it motivated us to keep pressing hard when times grew tough. Vision and mission are meant to work together. If you look back at both of our statements, you'll see two very important words that keep them bound as one: *so that*.

We believe those are two of the most powerful words in business. If you can write out *what* you want to accomplish in life and business, but you don't know *why*, then think deeply on that little phrase.

"I want to be (or achieve) _____
_____ [your *what*]

SO THAT I can _____
_____ [your *why*]."

We use this template when we coach entrepreneurs. It's simple, yet powerful.

Too many entrepreneurs fail in taking the time to craft a solid plan in this area. Some of them don't have their personal statements in place, so they end up winning in business but losing in relationships. Others know clearly what they want to accomplish in business but have no clue why, so they end up with a ton of success but little significance.

We don't want that to be your story. That's why step two in the Expert Ownership program includes clearly defining your vision and mission, both personally and professionally. When you do this, you'll discover that your daily tasks begin to align with the purpose God has for you.

And that is far more fulfilling than financial profit.

VALUES & PRINCIPLES

In baseball, knowing what you're swinging at and why you're swinging is great, but if you don't guide the bat to the right place, you won't hit the ball. In business, this is what values and principles help you do: They guide you on the path to accomplish your vision and mission.

Values define what's important to you. A value is typically one word that defines what you regard and treasure. While there are literally thousands of words that can define what you deem important, we strongly suggest narrowing it down to three to five words, both personally and professionally.

For us, our personal values were (and still are):

- Freedom
- Courage
- Strength
- Faithfulness

Everything we do centers on helping people in those areas. We want to ...

- See people experience freedom in their lives
- Strengthen those who are weak
- Help them stand with courage
- Enable them to be faithful in every area of life

For our real estate business, our values were:

- Faithful
- Honest
- Productive

- Speed
- Scale

We wanted to be ...

- Faithful to our clients by giving as much effort in the cheap properties as the expensive ones
- Honest by never cutting corners
- Produce amazing results ...
- ... Faster than all other vendors
- Scale to handle as many properties as banks could send our way

The last two points were derived from that conversation we had with Bill Spooner when he was impressed by our speed and wanted to know how many properties we could handle. Speed and scale became buzzwords in our office from then on. But we didn't want to just go fast and sell lots of properties without being faithful and honest.

Obviously, we value many other things, but these are the specific words we felt gave us the best chance to win in life and business.

While values are typically one-word descriptions of what you find most important, principles are short statements that tie those values to action.[23] Think of a bowtie: values are one part of the bow, and action is the other, yet they are tied together by the knot of principles.

Principles are statements that act as guides to where you're going and guardrails to keep you on the path. In our case, we used the same principles we derived for our personal lives in our business. Here they are:

---

[23] Ray Dalio, *Principles: Life and Work* (Simon and Schuster, 2017).

- Breathe life.
- Be a fountain, not a drain.
- Be a producer, not a consumer.
- Be faithful in little.
- Give more in value than you take in pay.

If you walked into our office back in the early 2000s, you would've seen these statements plastered all over our wall. In every interaction with every person—no matter if it was a customer or client, an outside contractor or vendor, a fellow employee or business partner—our goal was to operate within these principles. We knew if anyone representing Benham Real Estate Group did these five things, then we'd have a business we could be proud of.[24]

This was put to the test ten years into our business. Our largest client told us they had to bring on another broker in our area because of increased volume, and since we were top performers, they asked if we would train them ... for free. We remember sitting around a conference table with several of our managers, all of us knowing full well what we had to do. Our principles told us what to do in that moment—we weren't to think about what we could *get* as consumers, but what we could *give* as producers.

Yet the conversation was still a hard one. It's a tough pill to swallow when you have to give away some of your trade secrets (not all of them, mind you!).

But we knew if we stayed faithful in the little things, gave more value to our client than we took in pay, and thought about producing and not consuming, God would honor it and

---

[24] Feel free to use these principles as your own. The greatest compliment we could ever get is walking into the office of an entrepreneur we've coached and they have a few of our same principles plastered on their walls.

keep us at the top. By His grace, He did just that. We never saw a drop in our flow of inventory as a result of training that broker.

Do you see how important it is to define your values and principles? When things are good, your values and principles guide you on the right path. And when things are bad, they become guardrails to keep you from falling (or jumping) off!

TIE 'EM TOGETHER

Your vision and mission are born out of your values and principles. This is why the best business coaches in the world tell you to clearly define all of them. Later in the book, we'll show you how to incorporate each of these into your business plan.

Our good buddy, Casey Crawford, is a great example of how to properly use the Core Four. He's the founder of Movement Mortgage, the fastest-growing mortgage company in the world.

Casey is a believer whose goal is to see God glorified in his life through his business. To make sure his massive employee base stays on track to make that happen, he's written (in BIG letters) all over the walls of his sprawling campus the company *vision, mission, values, and principles.* By keeping those things out front, his company's worth has grown to well over a billion dollars.

Your company may pale in comparison to his (ours sure have), but the importance of clearly defining your *Core Four* will help you become the Expert Owner God wants you to become.

STEP THREE

IDEATION

_____

SeeYaPreneur

↗ 12. Money

/ 11. Leadership

/ 10. Team Building

/ 09. Systems

/ 08. Value Delivery

/ 07. Sales

/ 06. Marketing

/ 05. Value Creation

/ 04. Branding

/ **03. Ideation**

/ 02. Core Four

/ 01. Identity

CHAPTER TWELVE

IDEATION:
GENERATE YOUR IDEAS

So you've stepped up to the plate and the bat's in your hand. You've shifted your weight back, you've got your eye on the ball, you've started your swing by guiding your bat to the right place...

Now it's time to make contact.

But making contact in baseball is not the goal—*getting a hit* is. You can make contact all day long yet never find yourself running the bases. You've got to do what our grandpa used to say before our games: "Hit 'em where they ain't!" You've got to hit the ball to a spot on the field where an opposing player can't catch it. Only then do you have a chance to score. And when you score, you can win.

That's our goal for this chapter—to put you in a position to get a hit so you can score and win. And the way to do that is by generating creative IDEAS.

In the music and film industries, a good idea is called *a hit*. All the hits started as an idea that popped into someone's head, and when they put action to that idea, they ended up with a hit. They either created something original that nobody had thought of before or rearranged an original with a new twist. In either case, it started with a simple idea.

An entrepreneur, at the core, is someone who comes up with a unique idea and then executes to make it a reality. No matter where you are on the entrepreneurial road map, generating new ideas is the only way to get where you want to be.

Whether you're a wannapreneur who needs that first idea to start a new business, a solopreneur who needs an idea that will remove you from the day-to-day operations, or an entrepreneur who needs an idea to jump into another vertical, generating ideas is the lifeblood of business growth. When ideas stop, your business dies.

The question for us, then, is this: *How do we come up with good ideas?* And when we have one: *How do we know if we should act on it?* That's what we'll discuss in this chapter.

We separate this chapter into three sections:

- Unlocking the power of your brain.
- Looking for new ideas.
- Discerning if an idea is good for you.

I CAN ONLY IMAGINE

All good ideas start with your imagination. They begin with a thought of what *could* be and end with a desire for what *should* be. God made us with a unique ability to dream like this so we'd create awesome things as a reflection of what He did when He created everything.

When we were kids, we all did this instinctively, right? We grew up dreaming about what we wanted to do and who we wanted to be. The thought of "what could be" filled us with hope for a bright future and a passion to make it happen.

I (Jason) remember sitting on the curb out in front of our house as a kid, envisioning myself playing professional baseball. I usually ended up in our backyard taking swings off the tee. My imagination propelled me to action.

The problem is, as we get older and the routine of life sets in, we forget how to dream. And when that happens, we end up doing things that don't align with where we originally wanted to go.

To be successful in business, you must unlock the power of your imagination and learn to dream again. The imagination is a muscle; the more you use it, the more powerful and productive you'll become.

According to Josh Kaufman, author of the bestselling book *The Personal MBA*, "The imagination is the creative workshop of the mind that transforms your dreams into ideas and your ideas into reality."[25]

Leadership guru Simon Sinek echoed this when he said, "Success is when reality catches up to your imagination."[26]

Most people in business start with a dream, but quickly find themselves working so hard in the business they forget how to keep dreaming. As a result, they lack the creative energy needed to sustain and scale their company. They're so busy keeping the business afloat that they don't have the time to dream up new and exciting ideas.

Or they start out with the wrong idea—something that didn't fit who they were made to be—and now they're trapped in a business that's losing money and ruining their life. Or they're making money but have no meaning, and the passion is gone. They might have dreamed, but they didn't dream *well*.

We don't want that for you. We want you to use the power of your imagination to come up with good ideas that not only meet your needs and the needs of others but line up with the way you were created and wired so that you don't create

---

[25] Josh Kaufman, *The Personal MBA* (Portfolio, 2010).
[26] Simon Sinek, www.Facebook.com/SimonSinek

something that will suck the life out of you.

How do we do that? Well, you first have to unlock your brain!

UNLOCKING THE POWER
OF YOUR BRAIN

Did you know that your brain has a difficult time distinguishing between what you see with your eyes and what you see in your mind? We didn't either, until we read about a research project that measured brain activity in two groups of people—those who imagined a sunset and those who watched one in reality. Results showed the same brain activity taking place for both those who saw the real sunset and those who imagined it.[27]

That's crazy, right?

Have you ever seen someone in the middle of the mall at a virtual reality kiosk with glasses on as they stand awkwardly off-balance because they think they're about to fall off a cliff? Their bodies are simply reacting to what their brains think is real.

It works something like this: When you visualize something, your brain can't tell if it's real or not, so you begin to *feel* like it's real. This, then, taps into the power of your emotions.

And your emotions give you the impulse to act. When you *feel* something, it inspires you to *do* something. This is why virtual reality affects us the way it does.

Okay, now let's apply this concept to business—or even your life in general—because it's extremely powerful. The steps will look something like this:

[27] Travis Bradberry, *Emotional Intelligence 2.0* (Talentsmart, 2009).

1. You *visualize* yourself achieving your dream.

2. You then begin to *feel* like it's already real.

3. Engaging your emotions like this inspires you to think creatively.

4. As a result, you are motivated to do things that will make your dreams become reality.

This is why we wanted you to nail your vision right out of the gate. Having a vision—a picture in your head of what you want to achieve—begins to unlock the creativity within you.

This is what the two of us did when we first started our business.

I (David) remember calling Jason one Saturday afternoon while watching college football. "Dude," I said, "can you imagine what it would feel like to watch football on a Saturday if we both had our houses paid off, our business was running itself, and we had $2,500 a month in passive income coming in?"

"Yeah," he said. "Or if we could go to the park in the middle of the workday and push our kids on the swings without having to worry about money. That would be amazing."

Conversations like this were the norm for us, but it wasn't just "empty" dreaming. Visualizing where we wanted to be and what we wanted to accomplish tapped into our emotions; we began to *feel* like it was real before it actually was real. This unlocked the creative part of our brains (our imaginations), which in turn generated ideas to make those dreams a reality. As we were motivated to action, we took steps toward making our dreams come true.

Sounds good, you might say, *but how does it actually work?*

It works by tapping into your subconscious mind.

Your subconscious is at work 24/7 doing exactly what you tell it to do. How do you "tell" your subconscious mind to do something when it's … well … subconscious? You feed it instructions by visualizing what you want *as if it has already happened*. You don't even have to know how to get there because your subconscious will do a lot of the work. It does this by tapping into the reticular activating system (RAS) of your brain.[28] (That's a big word that makes us feel smart when we say it.)

The job of the RAS is to filter which thoughts from your subconscious make their way to the conscious mind. A person has something like fifty thousand thoughts a day. The vast majority of those thoughts remain beneath the level of conscious thought. They sit in your subconscious. If all those thoughts made their way to your conscious mind, your brain would literally short-circuit.

Have you ever bought a new car and then started noticing it everywhere, even though you never had before? That is your RAS at work. Once you set your intent on that specific car, your RAS notified your brain that it was significant. Now it triggers when you see it elsewhere. You can spot this car anywhere without trying. Before you activated the RAS, you never noticed that particular car even though it was there all along.

Let's circle back to how this applies in business. When you tell your brain that you want to be financially free, or you want to open twenty new locations, or you want to create a new stream of revenue for your business, anything that will make those things a reality will suddenly become significant.

---

[28] Chris Fox, in his book *5,000 Words Per Hour* (Chris Fox Writes LLC, 2015), discusses how the RAS helps you accomplish your dreams.

This means they will find their way into your conscious thoughts. And you'll begin to notice opportunities you never noticed before.

Famous comedian and actor Jim Carrey used the power of his imagination back in 1985 as he was starting out in Hollywood. He famously wrote himself a $10 million check for *acting services rendered*, dated it ten years in the future, and kept it in his wallet. A decade later, when he signed on for the lead role in *Dumb and Dumber*, guess how much his check was for? Ten million bucks![29]

By locking in and visualizing how you can meet a problem with a product or a service, your RAS will begin to identify the people, information, and opportunities that will help you achieve it. Solutions will literally be drawn to you like magnets.

So how can you use your RAS to generate ideas? We've discovered there are three steps to unlocking its power. You've got to:

1. Want it.

2. Focus on it.

3. Believe it.

It starts with a simple desire. How badly do you want it? If you want it, you'll start dreaming about it.

Then, focus on it … just like you focus on that new car you want to buy. Start paying attention. This is called *setting your intent*.

---

[29] Josh Hoffman, "Why Jim Carrey Wrote Himself a $10 million Check Before He had $10 Million," Medium.com, Jan. 7, 2019, https://medium.com/@socialmediajosh/why-jim-carrey-wrote-himself-a-10-million-check-before-he-had-10-million-3618090c9e

Finally, believe that you can achieve it. Don't give in to self-doubt. If you believe it—and it's God's will for your life—you can achieve it.

Utilizing these three steps is how we came up with every unique idea in our business (and our lives, for that matter). We thought of what we wanted, focused intently on getting it, and believed that we could achieve it.

We did this after talking with Rick Blinn in Starbucks, when we were on the verge of stepping out into franchising our business. Because we wanted to help him make money through selling bank-owned homes, we started focusing intently on how we could do it ... and we believed that we could achieve it, no matter the obstacles. The next thing we knew, ideas started flowing. Three years later, we were sitting at 100 offices sprawled across the U.S.

But here's one really important point: Before you use the power of your RAS, you've got to be anchored in the truth of God. If you don't have truth as your foundation, you'll end up using the power of your imagination to move you further from what God wants for you. For instance, a young man who wants to be a girl focuses on becoming a girl. Believing that he was born a girl is using his RAS to become something different than God made him to be. *(David: That's so politically incorrect!)*

When you stand upon truth as your foundation, there's no limit to what you can accomplish by using the incredible imagination God has given you. So, don't let yourself just glide through your day, oblivious to the world around you. Unlock your RAS and begin dreaming about the best solutions to meet felt needs!

Don't view the world as it is. View it as you would like it to be.

The founders of Uber sat in taxis just like we all have, but they utilized the power of their imagination to dream about what *should* be. And in time, they realized how it *could* be. You can do the same.

WHERE TO LOOK FOR IDEAS

As much as we love using our RAS, there is a downside. Even when you're anchored in God's truth, you might still dream up things that aren't in your core area of business and expertise. If you pursue this kind of dream, you'll find yourself traveling down a rabbit hole with no end in sight. You need to guide yourself to dream *the right way* if you're going to achieve your ultimate goals.

In other words, you don't just need to dream … you need to dream *well*.

When it comes to dreaming up a business idea, one of the best principles can be found in perhaps the greatest baseball movie of all time—*Field of Dreams*. If you've seen the movie, you already know the principle: "If you build it, they will come."

If you haven't seen the film, here's a quick summary: An Iowa farmer has a dream to build a baseball field for a group of epic ballplayers who'd been kicked out of the game decades before. He built it, and they magically showed up.

The movie taught us that your business isn't about you fulfilling *your* dream; it's about helping others fulfill *their* dream. A good business idea starts with the customer in mind. It doesn't start with *your* thing but with *their* thing, not with *your* need but with *their* need.

You can build a baseball diamond in a cornfield if that's your dream, but nobody's coming unless it's *their* dream. Tuning into what others need is a key to dreaming well.

A good business idea does one of two things:

1. Solves an unsolved problem

2. Brings a better solution to a problem that's already been solved

Just like we touched on earlier with your brain filter, you have to attune your thoughts in order to find solutions to people's problems. We call this *looking for problem pools*.

A *problem* is a frustration, inefficiency, or complaint in someone's life.

A *pool* is the number of people who share those problems.

If you can solve the problems of a pool, you have both a business *and* a market in which to sell. (We cover this more in detail in our chapter on Value Creation.)

When you identify a problem in a small enough pool, your RAS activates without you even knowing it. Ideas will begin flowing into your mind. God wired your brain this way.

You may not know it, but your brain is a problem-solving machine. When you focus on problems, solutions to those problems will manifest themselves.

For example, if we casually drop in 2+2=? here, your mind will instantly jump to the number 4. It can't resist solving that simple problem. If we made the problem more complicated, your brain might not give you the answer right away, but it would jump into problem-solving mode to figure out a solution.

Focusing on problem pools in this way will help you generate all sorts of ideas. The question then becomes, which of these should you activate?

FINDING YOUR SWEET SPOT

When you hit the ball *right on the nose* in baseball, we call it "hitting the sweet spot."

The sweet spot is the perfect place on the bat where you want to hit the ball every time—right in the middle of the barrel. When you hit the ball there, it's like you don't even feel it; it just explodes off the bat. Hitting the sweet spot allows the ball to travel the furthest with the least amount of effort.

As an entrepreneur, your sweet spot is the intersection between your passion, proficiency, profit, and purpose.[30]

Passion

Your passion is what you're excited about. It's what energizes you. Its motto is, "Do what you LOVE." Leadership coach Michael Hyatt says that without passion, all you'll be left with is boredom.[31]

But as all entrepreneurs know, you don't have to be passionate about the specific product or service you're offering. Like diapers or cleaning services, for example. None of us dream about a dirty baby bottom, and few of us are dying to grab a mop and get to work. But we can be passionate about giving new parents confidence in their baby's clean rear end, or about keeping homes clean for people's health.

The two of us felt more passionate about building a business, providing jobs, and leading people than we did about selling homes. Houses just happened to be our product. Our ultimate passion was to bless wannapreneurs and solopreneurs with an opportunity to build something of their own so they could

---

[30] Jim Collins in *Good to Great: Why Some Companies Make the Leap and Others Don't* (Harper Business, 2001)outlined the first three points of the sweet spot. We added the fourth.
[31] MichaelHyatt.com

impact their city (through our franchise). This passion drove us to build something big.

The key in business is to define your passion not by the specific product or service, but by *the opportunity to build something that can bless others.* We jumped at the opportunity to sell bank-owned homes, and the next thing you know, we had a burning passion to grow it big because we knew it could help a lot of people.

Ask yourself, "What am I passionate about? What do I want to accomplish with my life?"

Proficiency

Proficiency is about *talent* and *skill*—what you're good at. Its motto is, "Do what you do best."

There's a difference between talent and skill. Talent is the ability you are born with. Skill is what you learn along the way. The idea that you should only work in the area of your talent is hogwash. Learning new skills can help you generate the income you need. Then, you will hopefully reach the point of being able to hire others. And finally, the hope is that one day you will be able to operate solely in the area of your talent.

This is how we started out. We had to develop skills that were outside our talents (and our passions), yet we did it because we knew we could develop others to ultimately take over those jobs.

I (Jason) learned the skill of developing web apps early on. Talk about activating new pathways for the reticular activating system! There is not a single synapse in my body that thinks technologically, yet I understood that learning how to do this would give our business the best chance to scale nationally.

And that's what happened. After five years of strenuous skill development, we had a rock-star system managing all our locations nationwide. At that point, I handed the reins to someone else and have not thought about app development since.

Ask yourself, "What am I naturally good at? What can I learn to do that will help me grow my business and then hand it over to someone else?" Without proficiency, you'll fail at whatever you attempt.

Profitability

The third component of your sweet spot is profitability. Can you make money at it? Its motto is, "Do what makes cash." Without profitability, all you have is a hobby.

The desire to make money is not a bad desire. Actually, it's a *really good* desire. You just can't fall in love with it. God uses our desire for financial reward to be the thing that gets us moving in the right direction. Then, once you're moving in that direction, money no longer becomes the motivator—serving others does.

We never would have gotten into real estate if there wasn't the hope of making good money at it. But once we got in and we realized the lives we could impact by becoming proficient, that better motivation took over.

The problem comes when you allow a love for money to creep into your heart. When you begin to thirst for making money rather than changing lives, you'll find that you may become rich financially but flat broke relationally. You'll have plenty of cash but nobody to enjoy it with.

On the other hand, if you can't make money with your idea, then all you have is a hobby. If you want to hit your sweet spot in business, your idea needs to be something that can generate enough money to pay for itself. Otherwise, you're moving into the nonprofit space (which is also a noble profession if that's the direction you want to go).

Ask yourself, "Will this new idea make me money or ultimately cost me money?"

Purpose

The fourth component of your sweet spot is purpose. It asks the question, "Why am I alive?" Its motto is, "Do what you were made to do."

According to Psalms 139:16, you were created by God with a pre-packed purpose: "You saw me before I was born. Every day of my life was recorded in your book. Every moment was laid out before a single day had passed."

The last thing you want to do is make money and have fun doing it, only to lack a sense of fulfillment at the end of the day. When it comes to staying in your sweet spot, does the idea help you achieve your "why"?

The two business blunders we mentioned in an earlier chapter are great examples of what *not* to do in this regard. We knew deep down that getting involved with those businesses didn't align with our purpose of bringing life to communities nationwide. We did it anyway ... and ended up with more stress and less money. (That's a vicious combo)

Ideas can be good, but if there's not a compelling reason behind *why* you should do it, then mark it off your list.

Find the intersection of these four—passion, proficiency, profit, and purpose. This is your sweet spot. Your best ideas in business will find themselves aligning with each of these.

God wants you to get a hit in business. He wants you to score and win. And He's gifted you in a unique way to make it happen. When you unlock the power of your imagination and begin to dream again, like you did when you were a kid, just step up to the plate, take a swing, and watch what happens.

Tony Robbins may say, "Awaken the GIANT within," but we say, "Awaken the DREAMER within!" When you do this, you'll discover a host of ideas to start, sustain, and scale your business.

STEP FOUR

BRANDING

SeeYaPreneur

↗ 12. Money

／ 11. Leadership

／ 10. Team Building

／ 09. Systems

／ 08. Value Delivery

／ 07. Sales

／ 06. Marketing

／ 05. Value Creation

／ **04. Branding**

／ 03. Ideation

／ 02. Core Four

／ 01. Identity

CHAPTER THIRTEEN

BRANDING:
BUILD YOUR BRAND

If you wrap it right, they'll open it. This isn't about Christmas gifts or birthday presents—it's about your brand. If you aim for lasting success, you must learn to wrap your business and present it in such a way that makes people want to open up and see what's inside.

You may have the best idea in the world. You can transform it into a phenomenal product or service. But if you don't package it properly or position it right, then no amount of effort will get it into the hands of the people who need it most. At least, not as many people as you could if you *do it right*.

Many wannapreneurs go out and start marketing their idea the minute they come up with it, assuming the quality of what they're selling will set them apart. That might work if you want to remain a solopreneur, but it's not the path of the Expert Owner.

If you want to sell to the masses, to build a business where you move from wannapreneur to solopreneur to entrepreneur and eventually to SeeYaPreneur, *you've got to have a good brand.*

Marketing and sales are fun, but if you want to 10x your sales, you'll need to spend the time developing your brand so that it fits into a few key elements we already discussed:

- Who you are
- Why you do what you do

This is why we spent time discussing your *who, why, and what* right out of the gate. Once you have a clear picture of those critical components, you are ready to develop your brand.

So, what is a brand? Simply put, your brand is what people think and feel about your business. It's that image that is evoked when your company is mentioned ... that gut feeling a customer has when they think about your product or service.

Too many people in business confuse a brand with a logo. Logos are important, but your brand is far more significant and valuable than that. It's so valuable that the Coca-Cola brand alone is worth more than $84 billion—and that doesn't include the business or assets.[32]

Our brand is what initially caught HGTV's attention. They told us they were drawn not only by our reputation for excellence in real estate but also that we did it in a fun, family environment. Well, guess what! We built it that way *on purpose*.

But when activist groups found out that HGTV hired two guys with conservative values and biblical beliefs, they attacked the very thing they knew could take us down—our brand. They painted a fake news picture of us and published it to the world, repositioning our brand from successful entrepreneurs with a desire to help families succeed in real estate to right-wing, bigoted, hateful guys who deserved to have their show canceled.

Their plan worked. We got fired, and HGTV lost millions. All because an activist group branded us to the public before HGTV had their opportunity.

That's the power of a brand.

---

[32] Statista.com

When we first got into business, we didn't know anything about how powerful a brand was. Of course, we had been surrounded by brands our entire lives, but we never thought anything about it.

As kids, we had a picture of Michael Jordan on our wall with a Nike swoosh at the top, and the phrase *Just Do It* at the bottom. That poster inspired us to work hard at basketball and dunk like he did. It pulled us out of bed those early mornings to hit our leg routine, trying to get strong enough to jump like Mike.

Nike's brilliant use of its brand not only inspired us to work hard as athletes, but also to buy Nike products. It masterfully showed us that the best brands aim at your *internal* desire more than your *external* desire. Yeah, we wanted a pair of Nike shoes, but what we *really* wanted was to dunk like MJ and hear the crowd roar when we did it. Nike's branding showed us that owning those shoes could help us get there. Soon, we found ourselves dunking basketballs in brand new Air Jordan shoes (compliments of our grandpa).

That Nike poster hanging on our wall MOTIVATED us and MOVED us to action, which are the two things all good brands do:

- Motivate customers by appealing to their internal desire
- Move them to action by appealing to their external desire

Your external desire is your *felt* need. It's the conscious need or desire you feel in the moment. For us as kids, it was, "We need great basketball shoes."

Your internal desire is what's *truly* driving you. It's the unconscious need you feel inside. That need might be to feel accepted, loved, approved, to feel a sense of accomplishment, etc. For us, it was tied to acceptance and accomplishment: "We want to hear the crowd cheer for us when we dunk like MJ in a game."

It works much the same way for our wives every holiday season. At Thanksgiving, they talk a lot about the food they need to buy for our feast. The desire to buy food is the *felt* need. But their real desire isn't for us to taste good food; it's to have our families enjoy time together and connect on a deeper level. Having good food is the external desire that gives them an opportunity to fulfill their internal desire.

This is why commercials from grocery stores around the holidays don't just feature an amazing turkey that makes your mouth water; they show a family sitting around a table enjoying each other's company. The external desire (food) is secondary to the internal desire (connecting with family). That's good branding (and marketing, which delivers your brand—but we'll talk about that in another chapter).

There's a lot we can cover on brand. Entire books have been written about the subject. But we want to make it very simple for you. As we've built our companies over the years and coached other entrepreneurs, we've boiled brand into three critical components:

- Mark
- Message
- Meaning

Looking back at Nike's branding for the poster on our wall. Its Mark is what we saw with our eyes—its logo, colors, pictures, etc.

Its Message was this: "You know you want to dunk a basketball; now just go out and do it." Of course, that's not exactly what the words said, but that's the message we heard when we saw the poster.

The Meaning behind its Mark and Message was, "You can crush every obstacle in front of you and accomplish your dream in sports. White men CAN jump!"

It was seamless and inconspicuous. They didn't have to tell us their Meaning; they got us to *feel* it. The more we looked at that poster in our room with the swoosh, the slogan, and a picture of Jordan flying through the air in his killer kicks, the more hooked we became.

So let's get practical and talk about each of these individually. We'll start with the most important of all: Meaning.

WHAT DO YOU MEAN?

Your Meaning is your company identity. It's who you are as a business, what you represent, and why you do what you do. This is why we covered mission, vision, and values before we jumped into brand.

Your Mark and Message stand upon the foundation of your Meaning. You've got to spend time thinking through this before you start creating logos, choosing colors, selecting images, and crafting messages.

Nike's mission statement is "to bring inspiration and innovation to every athlete in the world."[33] This is what defines its Meaning. Although it doesn't necessarily broadcast that phrase in its ads, the consistent use of their Mark and Message clearly lines up with Nike's Meaning.

Your Meaning tells people WHY they should buy from you. *When their why lines up with your why, they will buy.* Research shows that 87 percent of people will purchase solely because

---

[33] Nike.com

of brand values.[34] So getting clear on your Meaning is the first step to ensuring that people will buy from you.

Your customers are looking for solutions to their deepest problems. But as we said earlier, their external need is not what's truly driving them. A good brand knows this and taps into that internal desire in a way that motivates people and moves them to action.

Every person has five basic human needs:

1. Security

2. Identity

3. Belonging

4. Purpose

5. Competence

We'll dive into each of these concepts in our chapter on leadership. But for now, just know that tapping into one or more of these core needs is what gives your brand meaning. When you make someone feel safe or accepted for who they are, when you help them feel like they belong, that they are called to a higher purpose, or that they are able to achieve something great, customers will be drawn to your brand.

How do you know your customers' internal needs? You start by asking the simple question, "What do my customers *really* want?" Knowing that there's a deeper desire behind their felt need will guide you in the right direction and define the meaning behind your brand.

---

[34] "2017 Cone Communications CSR Study," https://www.conecomm.com/research-blog/2017-csr-study

Then ask, "How can I give them what they want? What's unique about me (or my product) that can meet their internal desires?"

God made you unique for a purpose. This is your opportunity to use your uniqueness to help others. Or, as my (Jason's) father-in-law says, "God wants to use the uniqueness of you to present the uniqueness of Him."

When we got to know our first client, Bill Spooner, we learned quickly that his job was high stress with lots of turnover and few promotions. His external desire was to sell the houses in his portfolio. But his true desire, the one he had deep inside, was job security. Everything in our branding to asset managers from that point forward centered on this. We wanted them to feel that using our services would lower their stress, provide job security, and help them get promoted.

> One quick note ... at this point we had zero experience in branding, but we were spending time daily in prayer and Bible reading. During those times, God spoke to us about meeting the *real* needs of our clients and not just the needs of the moment. God guided us to do these things before we even discovered that the best brands did them. This is the value of partnering with God in your business: He will always guide you to do the right thing if you give Him an opportunity to work with you.

Our Benhambrand started taking on new meaning as word spread fast amongst asset managers. We became the go-to guys for hundreds of them, all of whom had the same internal desire that Bill Spooner had. By tapping into their internal desire, we were able to create a corporate identity that attracted clients to us.

Our business partner and renowned brand strategist, Larry Hubatka, says that the number one goal in branding is to make your customer feel as though they can "become" something by choosing to hire you. For us, we focused on helping asset managers feel as though they could "become" more successful at their job, less stressed at home, and have more fun at the office because we would do the heavy lifting for them. Everything we did with our branding—the things they saw and heard—revolved around these things.

Our good friend, Ian Pratt, taught us that the key to developing a good brand is to *know yourself, know your customer, and connect the two*. By connecting the two, you consistently and clearly communicate how you are helping solve the customer's problem.[35] When your Meaning is built around meeting the internal needs of your customers, connecting the two will flow naturally.

This is where your Mark and Message come into play. Consistently using both of these is how you convey your Meaning to the masses.

MARK IT UP

While your Meaning is your *identity*, your Mark is your *identifier*. It consists of your name, logo, pictures, colors, fonts—everything that's visual and doesn't include words. Nike's white swoosh on a dark black background, or placed on a bright orange box, looks like a checkmark … like you've just completed a difficult task and can now check it off the list. But much more elegant. No words, all visual.

---

[35] Ian founded Weller Creative and helped us craft the brand for Expert Ownership. He talked extensively about branding on ExpertOwnershipLive. com

Research reveals that people make a subconscious judgment about a person, environment, or product within ninety seconds of initial viewing, and between 62 percent and 90 percent of that assessment is based on color alone.[36] Taking the time to think through the visuals of your business so they line up with your Meaning is of extreme importance.

We're not designers by any stretch, so when it came to branding our first company, we hired a group to handle it for us—and we're glad we did. Creating a visual brand requires creative minds to be involved. If that's not you, don't even attempt to do it on your own. (And if you don't have the money to spend on a good design, please wait until you can.)

There are four critical components to creating your brand Mark in a way that will clearly communicate your brand meaning. All of your pictures, colors, logos, fonts, etc. need to be:

1. Simple

2. Memorable

3. Unique

4. Quality

If we said the word "Apple," what would you think? An apple with a bite taken out of it, perhaps?

An apple is simple. A bite mark makes that apple memorable. It's unique because no one else uses that image. And its quality is top notch. This is one of the reasons Apple has such a successful company; they have a simple, memorable brand image that evokes the idea of quality in the mind of the customer.

---

[36] Jill Morton, "Why Color Matters," Colorcom, https://www.colorcom.com/research/why-color-matters

We've been through three iterations of our Benham "B." Each time, we've tweaked things for the need of the moment. You can see our current iteration by downloading our Benham Brothers app. And we've always used the color blue because it's considered a "trust" color.

We never knew there was psychology involved in colors, but there is. Colors affect us physiologically and create emotions in us just by seeing them. Blue conveys trust, responsibility, calm, and stability.[37] And since this is exactly what we wanted our target customers to feel about us, we chose it for our brand.

Your Mark is the setup for your Message. It visually engages people to a point where they want to know what you're all about. We cannot stress enough how important it is that you take the time and spend the money to nail your visuals, because nobody is going to hear your Message if you don't.

WHAT'S YOUR MESSAGE?

Your Message consists of the words, phrases, and slogans that are consistent with your brand. It should answer very clearly, and as succinctly as possible, these five questions:

1. Who are you?

2. What do you do?

3. What makes you different?

4. Why does it matter?

5. What should I do?

---

[37] Graham Watson, co-founder of We Can Creative, shared this in an article in *The Guardian*. August, 2015. https://www.theguardian.com/small-business-network/2015/aug/24/how-pick-colour-scheme-for-brand

If we were to put all of that into a paragraph for use in one of our coaching companies, it would sound something like this:

"Hi, we're the Benham brothers. We train high-powered entrepreneurs how to serve God, achieve financial independence, and make an impact that lasts. We've generated hundreds of jobs around the world and provided thousands of dollars for those in need while becoming independently wealthy at the same time. We believe you can do the same, and we're going to show you how. Sign up below for a free consultation."

We told you who we are and what we do. Then we told you what makes us different—that we don't just own businesses but that we leverage them to help people and make an impact. Then we make an appeal to the "giver" inside every entrepreneur: "You can do the same!"

That gets them saying, "Yes! I want to have an impact like that." We end with a simple call to action.

Your branding encapsulates this without saying all that. You're not going to see that paragraph written on anything that we have. The goal is to develop your brand in a way that people hear it and feel it without you having to say it like that.

Let's go back to Nike again. Its mission is to "bring inspiration and innovation to every athlete in the world." But it doesn't put this on all its boxes and posters or say it in its commercials. What it does do is show its mark and give its message—whatever that message is for the specific ad. Then it slaps a picture of a world-famous athlete in there to let you know it's legit.

That's it. Combine that with its name and colors, and Nike has one incredibly cohesive and powerful brand, chock full of meaning.

When you consistently use your Mark and your Message, showing how you bring value to your target customers and can help them solve their problems, you will slowly but surely establish your Meaning. People will start to "get" you. They will begin to like you. And best of all ... they will trust you.

Why? Because they know instinctively that you won't just help them with their need for the moment, but you will help them fulfill that deeper longing inside. That's the power of a brand.

WRAP IT RIGHT

Before we close this chapter, we want to give you six practical steps to build your brand. Following them will help you sharpen your brand and enable you to attract the masses.

STEP 1 - Define Your Target Customer (or Client)

Ask yourself, what is their ...

- Age
- Location
- Stage of life

Additionally, what are their ...

- Spending patterns
- Values
- Desires
- Interests

The more specific you get in detailing your target customer, the ideal client, the better. We'll talk more about this in the next chapter.

STEP 2 - Focus On What Will Attract Them

What do they want the most? What would make their life better? How can you paint a picture that would inspire them to buy your product?

Focus on these wants and desires as you craft your brand image.

STEP 3 - Clarify Visuals and Voice

What do they like to see and how do they like to hear it?

For example, if you're in the relationship business and you help newlyweds handle conflict, you'll most likely want softer visuals and more of an encouraging *counselor* voice, rather than bold visuals and a harder *coaching* voice. But if you're in the fitness space and you specialize in bootcamps, then unleash your inner lion!

As a rule of thumb, the more *personal* you are, the stronger your brand. Customers like to know the people behind the business.

STEP 4 - Create a Slogan

Write a short tagline that is easy to remember. One of the best ways to generate ideas for a slogan is to start with "We believe …"

If we had been in the Nike brainstorming sessions helping to create its world-famous slogan, someone might have thrown out, "We believe people can become elite athletes if they're willing to just do it."

Then another person might have chimed in, "I like that— JUST DO IT! That's our slogan."

STEP 5 - Brand Hack

This is the fun part, because generating original ideas is not the work of pure genius—anyone can do it. To help you get kick-started down the right path, start by researching your top three competitors.

Look at their websites, their social media accounts, their funnels and ads—everything. Write down what you like best.

Then find the top three of your favorite brands outside your market and do the same with them. What works? What doesn't? Make a list and get it ready for your brand developer. He (or she) will thank you for it.

STEP 6 - Create a Brand Guide

This is important because it will become the roadmap for all your branding assets in the future. Your brand guide will ensure that your mark, message, and meaning are cohesively communicated to your customers.

It will also become a part of your business system that will ultimately free you from your business altogether. We'll talk more about that in our chapter on Systems.

So, that's branding in a nutshell.

In summary, when it comes to your product or service, if you wrap it right, they'll open it. You don't have to be a brand expert, you just need a quality Mark, a consistent Message, and a powerful Meaning that gives your target customer a good gut feeling that lets them know they can trust you … and ultimately buy from you.

How fun is that?

STEP FIVE

VALUE CREATION

SeeYaPreneur

↗ 12. Money

/ 11. Leadership

/ 10. Team Building

/ 09. Systems

/ 08. Value Delivery

/ 07. Sales

/ 06. Marketing

/ **05. Value Creation**

/ 04. Branding

/ 03. Ideation

/ 02. Core Four

/ 01. Identity

CHAPTER FOURTEEN

VALUE CREATION:
DESIGN YOUR PLAN

Okay, we've covered a few foundational business-building elements over the past few chapters. Here's a quick list to orient you as to where we are now:

1. You've got a firm understanding of who you are and the unique way God has gifted you to bless the world.

2. You know why you exist and what you'd like to accomplish with your life and business.

3. You've got a good business idea that people like (or *will* like).

4. You've grasped the importance of a solid brand.

You're now ready to put pen to paper and make this dream a reality!

Step Five is when you move from *mindset* to *movement* in your business-development process and you start the ball rolling toward making money off your idea. This step is all about *value creation*.

Value creation is about defining your value in a logical sequence and developing a plan around that proposition. If you're a wannapreneur or solopreneur, this chapter will help you discover ways you can bring value to your customers and how to craft a plan to follow in the months and years to come. If you're an entrepreneur with an existing business, this chapter will help you think through ways to expand what you currently offer and sharpen your existing plan so that it's simple and streamlined.

We cannot emphasize enough how important it is to have a well-written value proposition and detailed plan for your business. They act as a map to guide you to your ultimate destination ... like a set of blueprints for a house.

I (David) remember when I built my house several years ago. When I'd check on its progress, I'd often find the general contractor standing at the back of his truck with a host of sub-contractors looking over his shoulder as he showed them the blueprints. Nobody did anything without first consulting the plan to make sure that, when it was all said and done, I had the house we'd designed.

Can you imagine my contractor trying to build a house without these plans? It would be utter chaos. None of his sub-contractors would know what to do, and they'd get so frustrated at the confusion they'd probably walk off the job. All the while he'd feel stressed every single day—probably to the point where he'd consider checking himself into a psych ward. He'd be losing money, his family life would suffer, his kids would never see him, and the only time he'd have to himself would be during a shower ... and even then, he wouldn't be able to stop thinking about what he needed to do next.

And to top it all off, my own wife probably wouldn't talk to me anymore because we'd still be living in my parents' basement! Not her (or my) idea of success.

As foolish as it sounds to build a house without a plan, many people try to run their business that way. Or maybe they have a plan, but it wasn't well thought out and hasn't been shaped to fit their current environment. Or they developed a great plan at the start, but they're so busy working *in* their business that they have no time to actually work *on* the business by tweaking their plan.

But you don't have to be one of those people. There are three actions that fit under the main step of value creation. These three steps will help you make sure you won't be stuck without a plan when it matters most to your business:

- Describe Your Value
- Develop Your Ladder
- Detail Your Plan

You'll remember from our discussion on branding that all people are fueled by an internal desire that goes beyond their external desire. While your branding is aimed at your customer's deeper internal need, your value proposition, value ladder, and business plan are built solely for their external *felt* need.

DESCRIBE YOUR VALUE

The first thing you're going to do is describe the value you bring to the table. This is called your *value proposition*. It answers the overarching question, "What tangible value am I going to give the people who need what I can give them?"

An easy way to get started is by asking two key questions:

- Who are my dream customers?
- What results am I going to give them?

You've already been thinking about these questions from your work on branding. Now it's time to laser focus and pinpoint exactly what you're going to give them.

This is the way we crafted our value proposition for our first company. When Bill Spooner called us, elated over our speedy service, we knew exactly what he valued most. We made him our dream customer and detailed a plan to give him exactly what he wanted. Ten years later, we had sold more than thirty-two thousand houses for clients just like Bill.

A value proposition is a simple statement that summarizes why a customer would choose your product or service. It should easily explain why you exist. We are fans of Steve Blank's simple method for creating a value proposition:

We help (X) do (Y) by doing (Z).[38]

Our value proposition was simple: *We alleviate headaches for asset managers by managing and selling their foreclosed houses with speed and scale.* Speed and scale were the two things we knew our target customers wanted the most.

You can make your proposition as detailed as you'd like. But remember, it's best to keep it simple.

As your business grows you may have several different value propositions, depending on the market segment. Our franchise had this value proposition: *We help real estate agents succeed by training them to sell foreclosures and leveraging our relationships with existing banks.*

When it comes to defining or refining your value proposition, it's best to narrow it down as much as possible to focus on a specific niche within your market. The best way to make money is to bring value in the niches. The smaller the niche, the greater your chance for success.

---

[38] Steve Blank, "How to Build a Web Startup—Lean LaunchPad Edition," Sept. 22, 2011, https://steveblank.com/2011/09/22/how-to-build-a-web-startup-lean-launchpad-edition/

According to Russell Brunson, founder of ClickFunnels and all-around digital marketing guru, the most common markets fall into one of these three categories: Health, Wealth, or Relationships.[39] Each of these markets have submarkets. Yet the real money isn't found in the market or submarket; it's found in the niches. The riches are in the niches.

For us, it worked like this:

- Our market was Wealth.
- Our submarket was Real Estate.
- Our niche was Foreclosures.

But we took it a step further and moved into what we call a *hyper-niche* when we decided to franchise our model to other agents in the same space. From there, we kept drilling down to find additional ways to solve problems for banks and the agents who served them. Drilling down like this helped make our niche smaller and our value proposition stronger.

Years later, we accomplished the same thing in the nonprofit space as we partnered with a missionary friend in the Philippines who wanted to offset his need to raise financial support. He was a former college football player and had an interest in fitness, so we started a CrossFit gym.

- The market was Health.
- The submarket was Exercise.
- The niche was CrossFit.

We developed a plan, delivered on that plan, and in the end, he was able to sell that gym and buy a piece of land that now

---

[39] Russell Brunson, *Expert Secrets: The Underground Playbook for Creating a Mass Movement of People Who Will Pay for Your Advice* (Morgan James Publishing, 2017).

houses an orphanage called Safe Haven.[40] Our missionary friend runs it and is helping other missionaries start businesses the same way. Exciting times!

DEVELOP YOUR LADDER

Once you've defined your value proposition inside your niche, it's time to develop your value ladder. Digital entrepreneurs have used the value ladder for the last few decades, but it's rapidly catching on outside the digital space.

A value ladder is a method of mapping out your product/ service offering *visually* in ascending order of value and price. The value ladder allows you to cater to your client's needs no matter where they are in the customer journey.[41] Developing a value ladder helps you to break your value proposition into simple steps to keep customers in your ecosystem. The steps look something like this:

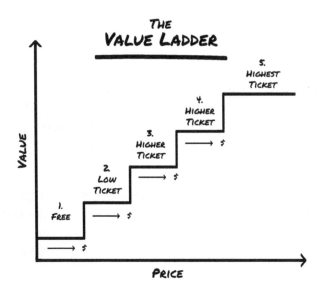

---

[40] Safe Haven Kids, https://www.facebook.com/SafeHavenKidsPH/
[41] Russell Brunson does a great job describing this.

1. You start by offering something that is free.

2. Then you sell a low-ticket product or service.

3. Your goal is getting the customer to buy a higher-ticket product ...

4. And then a higher one ...

5. Until they've reached your highest-ticket product or service.

Many businesses that you interact with on a day-to-day basis have value ladders, even if they've never actually called it that or written it down. Our dentist is one such guy. He starts out with a free checkup. When you go in for your checkup, he offers a low-priced cleaning, then a higher-priced whitening, then repairs, and finally cosmetic dental work—which is his highest-priced service.

You see how that works? Start with something free and move the customer through your value ladder to your highest-priced product or service.

A CrossFit gym works much the same way. It starts with a free class. Then there's a small drop-in fee of $10 per class, nutrition consulting for $75, a fundamentals class for $150, and then personal training starting at $250. Ultimately, however, the goal is to get you into their monthly membership program of $175 a month.

The ultimate goal in your value ladder is to get people into a membership program where they pay you consistently to be a part. It's called CONTINUITY—where you make money on a consistent basis through a membership program. We believe this is the new face of business. It's how fitness gyms, digital media companies, and others have made their bread and butter for years, and it's now rapidly expanding into many other industries.

No matter where they end up on your ladder—even if they don't buy your highest-priced product or service—you want them in your membership program. This will give you strength as a business, knowing you can count on a certain amount of money coming in every month, or quarter, or year.

Now, not every business can have a membership program. We get it. We don't want to pay our mechanic or local grocery store or favorite restaurant every month either. But they can all still have a value ladder that meets the needs of their customers right where they are.

But for a lot of other small businesses, we advise them to craft a value ladder with the goal of continuity if they want to stay ahead. Doing this not only gives you one-time income from sales but recurring revenue as well. And as anyone who's been in business can tell you, recurring revenue is king! You'll be surprised at how creative you can be when you start thinking this way.

Our dentist friend has a membership plan where we pay $250 a year for two cleanings and unlimited teeth whitening. That's continuity. *(David: I'm not sure the teeth whitening is working for Jason.)*

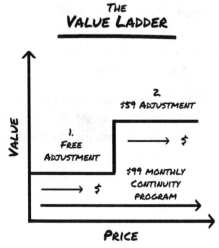

THE
VALUE LADDER

A friend of ours, who is a chiropractor, is using a continuity value ladder technique as well. She does one free adjustment, $59 per adjustment after that, or $99 a month for unlimited adjustments. Seems like a steal of a deal, right? But she realizes (rightly) that recurring revenue wins in the long run when it comes to keeping her doors open.

Our landscaper does the same thing. He charges us a monthly rate to take care of our office lawn. Gone are the days of charging per cut (like the two of us did back when we mowed lawns). Every lawn service out there would rather have you pay them monthly than by the service. Why? Because recurring revenue is better than one-time revenue. In business, continuity is king.

We have several friends in the fitness space who turned their personal training practices into monthly revenue generators by doing individualized programming for a low monthly rate. Each of them told us they are making more money with less financial headache than per-session payments.

Now, we're even seeing big companies like Disney jump into the continuity game. Disney+ chose to release its remake of *Lady and the Tramp* only to customers who were enrolled in their monthly membership program. This is a movie that would've easily crushed it in the box office. But box-office sales represent one-time purchases. Disney chose to break the box and go after recurring revenue.

As a result, it had ten million subscribers on day one, many of whom wanted to see that movie. At their opening price of $6.99 per month or $69 a year, you can do the math. Rather than a family going to the theatre and paying $70 to see one movie, they could now see that movie and any other Disney movie for $70 a year!

It was a brilliant move where everybody wins ... and Disney now has a massive base of customers it can count on to pay for its offerings over and over and over, like clockwork.

Panera Bread has even jumped into the game, offering an $8.99 monthly subscription for unlimited coffee. We have several friends who are loving every minute of that program!

The list of possibilities for your business is endless. The goal is continuous, consistent revenue coming in from your customers. It really is an amazing model. All it takes is a little creativity and a lot of determination, and you can create a value ladder that leads people into your continuity program.

For us in real estate, the road was a little more difficult. But in time, we figured out a way to do it. You can ALWAYS figure out a way!

Our value ladder looked like this:

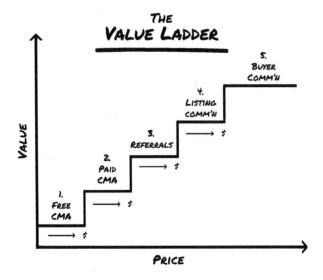

1. Free CMAs (comparative market analysis that shows the value of a house) - $0

2. Paid CMAs (for banks that needed them fast) - $50

3. Referrals from other brokers - $750–$2,500

4. Listing commission - $2,500–$5,000

5. Buyer commission - $3,500–$10,000+

Buyer commission was our highest-ticket item because listing commissions were typically discounted by the banks. But our goal was continuity, which was pretty much non-existent in the foreclosure brokerage space.

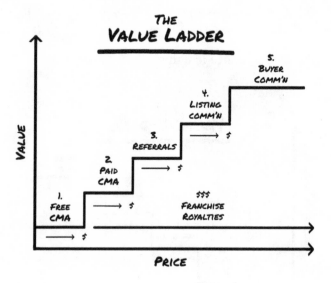

How did we do it?

We crafted a franchise model where brokers would pay us monthly and annually to be a part of our system. Up to that point, nobody had ever thought of doing what we did. But our strong desire for continuity unlocked our imagination, and the ideas started flowing. Ultimately, we crafted a plan that made millions.

But we didn't spend those millions on ourselves—we invested them to turn our cash into *cash flow*! (More on that later.)

We firmly believe that establishing your value ladder will help you thrive as a business more than just about anything else. Too often, we see businesses offering just one mid-tier or high-tier service or product without anything free or low-priced. That's like asking someone to jump up on a fifteen-foot platform. You need to give them steps to get there. That's what the value ladder does.

Don't ever underestimate the power of offering something for free. Not only have countless studies been done that show offering a free product moves people from interest to action, but it also puts their contact information into your personal database. This allows you to build a list of prospects that you "own"—you don't have to pay to advertise to them or pay to buy a list. The bigger your list, the more revenue you can generate.

But the best part of having a large list of people is that you can build relationships with them. This is how you can gain a loyal base of people who will buy whatever you sell. As you contact them consistently and add value to their lives, they will grow to trust you, like you, and even love you.

Okay, so maybe you don't have a value ladder, but you just realized how much you need one. Or maybe you already have several different products or service levels, but you need a few more. Or you want to start a continuity program. Whatever it is and wherever you are, take the time to fill out your ladder.

Write it down! This is a valuable part of the business planning process.

And remember—there's no right or wrong number of steps in your ladder. You may only offer two levels of service along with something free, or you may have ten levels. It doesn't matter. What matters is that you break your value proposition down into steps and find a way to get people into your continuity program. That's the goal.

DETAIL YOUR PLAN

Now that you know your value proposition and have your ladder in place, it's time to get to the business of writing out your plan. The four scariest words in business are: *Write a business plan!* The idea alone is enough to make people shudder.

We're not joking here. When it comes to business planning, we've seen four different types of people:

- Those who don't have a plan.
- Those who have one but don't act on it.
- Those who have a plan and act on it, but don't check it consistently and revise.
- Those who have one, act on it, and check it consistently to make revisions as necessary.

It doesn't take a degree in rocket science to know which category consistently hits the ball out of the park. We want *you* to be in this fourth category. You'll have a much better chance at succeeding in your business if you are.

And no, you don't need to break out in a cold sweat at the thought of creating a detailed plan that is dozens of pages long. When we first started in business, we realized the wisdom behind the one-page business plan. It kept things simple and actionable. But as we grew and saw God's hand working in our business, we added a valuable second page.

And with our *Two Page Plan*, we built every company we currently have.

One quick caveat: if you're seeking outside funding, a one or two-page plan will not suffice to secure those funds. A plan like that is beyond the scope of this chapter. But even if you do require something more robust, we still advise you to have the two-pager we're about to show you.

The first page of our *Two Page Business Plan* includes six simple components:

- Vision
- Mission
- Goals
- Strategies
- Money
- Action Plan

Condensing all of this to one page will keep you hyper-focused and not allow you to get bogged down. Having to sift through too many words will create analysis paralysis. Those are curse words to an Expert Owner.

Fortunately, you already defined your vision and mission when you wrote out your Core Four. So all you'll have to do is copy and paste them into your plan. (See, we told you it would be simple!)

Let's look at each of these individually. We'll use our real estate company as an example.

VISION—*What are you building?* Describe in detail what it is you're trying to do.

Our vision: "To become the premiere foreclosure brokerage in the nation."

MISSION—*Why are you building it?* What reason do you have for building your business?

Our mission: "To inspire a culture of life in communities across the nation."

GOALS—*What will you accomplish with your business?* When writing goals, we use the *SMARTER* system: Specific, Measurable, Achievable, Relevant, Time-Bound, Evaluated on a regular basis, and Rewarded when achieved.[42]

We listed only three goals at the start: Gross revenue, number of clients, and number of properties.

When it comes to goals, remember this: *A dream written down is a goal, but a goal broken down is a plan.* Start with your dream and then work from there to make it into a plan.

STRATEGIES—*How will you do it?* A strategy is a plan of action designed to achieve a major or overall aim.[43] This is where you get really specific with your plan.

Entrepreneurial guru Gino Wickman calls this phase "writing out your rocks." It refers to writing down the three to seven most important things you need to get done in the next ninety days.[44]

Here are a few of the strategies (rocks) we had when we first started our real estate company:

- Build out two new creative solutions in our value ladder to bring in extra revenue.
- Take three trips to visit out-of-state clients.

---

[42] Michael Hyatt is the first person we read who taught the SMARTER goal system.

[43] Dictionary.com

[44] Gino Wickman, *Traction: Get a Grip on Your Business* (BenBella Books, 2012).

- Attend two industry conferences.
- Create an Excel spreadsheet that can ultimately be turned into an online system.

Each quarter when we'd review our plan, we'd change the strategies necessary for the upcoming quarter.

MONEY—*How much will you make?* Project revenue and expenses—money in and money out.

We kept ours simple: Bring in $100,000 GCI (gross commission income) a month at a 30 percent margin. Of course, the income number grew each quarter. But the goal was always to keep our fixed and variable expenses less than 70 percent of revenue. (That's a hefty profit margin, but you can do that in real estate.)

ACTION PLAN—*What are your next steps?* This is your to-do list as a business (not your personal to-do list).

One of our first thirty-day action plan lists looked like this:

- Contact twenty-five prospective bank clients.
- Contact each existing client at least one time for something other than business.
- Hire a new assistant for admin tasks.
- Train someone to take over valuations.
- Create a process checklist for offers and closings.

Now let's look at the second page of the plan. This page is by far the most important. It contains one simple, but extremely powerful, component:

- Listening Prayer

We cannot overstate the importance of incorporating God's voice into your business plan. When you make it a habit to get up early and listen to your Business Partner (God) He'll reveal things to you that you never would've known any other way. He does this because He wants to teach you to rely on Him, like George Müller did when he built his massive organization.

God has all the answers to every problem you could ever have in business. And He'll tell you exactly what you need to do to meet the needs of your customers and clients. You just need to learn how to listen to Him. Page two of your business plan is devoted to doing just that.

This page is for you to write down what God speaks to you in the secret place—that quiet place where you're alone with Him, listening for His voice. And when He speaks to your heart, write it down! In this way He will direct you in your business.

So that's it for detailing your plan. Each time you review your two-page plan, you can change things as necessary. We'd suggest transferring what you wrote on page two into an ongoing prayer journal to make space for God to continue to speak. Your goal should be to *review your plan at least once a month* (if you can do it once a week, even better). This will keep you consistent and accountable.

Now you've targeted your market, narrowed it down into a niche, and discovered what they wanted. Armed with your **value proposition**, your **value ladder**, and your **two-page business plan**, you're ready to take this game to the next level!

SeeYaPreneur

↗ 12. Money

/ 11. Leadership

/ 10. Team Building

/ 09. Systems

/ 08. Value Delivery

/ 07. Sales

/ **06. Marketing**

/ 05. Value Creation

/ 04. Branding

/ 03. Ideation

/ 02. Core Four

/ 01. Identity

CHAPTER FIFTEEN

MARKETING:
CAPTURE YOUR LEADS

Once you've defined your value proposition, developed your value ladder, and crafted your two-page business plan, it's time to *test the market* with your product or service.

Your ultimate goal at this point is to bring people through what we call our three-phase upcycle. As you work to become an Expert Owner, you will learn to move people through these three phases seamlessly:

- From *prospects*
- To *purchasers*
- To *promoters*

Over the next three chapters, we'll cover each of these in turn. Marketing is all about gaining *prospects*. Sales converts those prospects into *purchasers*. Value Delivery turns purchasers into *promoters*.

First, we'll look at marketing. Ideally, marketing isn't a step in the process of building your business, but something that's built into every communication, product, and experience you offer.

Effective marketing begins in the branding phase and carries all the way through the sale and beyond. Fortunately, you've already developed your brand identity, so you know who you are and what you offer—now you just have to take your value proposition to the market.

One definition of marketing we agree with defines it as "the deliberate communication of value, intended to influence consumer decisions."[45] The aim of marketing is to arouse desire in your target customer so they want what you offer.

It's easy to confuse marketing and sales. Here are some ways we differentiate between the two:

Marketing is about lead *capture*. Sales is about lead *conversion*.

Marketing captures *eyeballs*. Sales captures *wallets*.

Marketing gains *leads*. Sales gains *buyers*.

When the rubber meets the road and you get into the day-to-day marketing and sales of your product or service, you can't really tell one from the other. They seamlessly blend into each other. But for purposes of our program, we keep the two separate.

There's a four-step formula that nearly every marketing strategy in the last century has utilized, even if unintentionally. Back in the 1880s, a man by the name of Elias St. Elmo Lewis founded an advertising agency. When gaining prospects and moving them to purchasers, he saw a recurring pattern and developed it into a strategy now widely known as the AIDA model.[46]

A stands for *Attention*. It answers the question, "Who are you?" The customer says, "I SEE it."

I stands for *Interest*. It answers the question, "What do you offer?" The customer says, "I LIKE it."

---

[45] Marquis Matson, "What is Marketing, Anyway?" A Working Definition," ReferralCandy Blog, https://www.referralcandy.com/blog/what-is-marketing/.
[46] Lewis was attributed the AIDA model in Edward K. Strong Jr.'s book, *Psychology of Selling and Advertising* (McGraw-Hill Book Company, 1925).

D stands for *Desire*. It answers the question, "Why should I buy?" The customer says, "I WANT it."

A stands for *Action*. It answers the question, "How can I get it?" The customer says, "I'll BUY it."

This little AIDA formula has been repeated over and over in businesses across the globe ever since Lewis came up with it. Grab their attention, gain their interest, spark their desire, move them to action. An Expert Owner knows how to position his or her product or service so that people *see it, like it, want it*, and *buy it*.

While it's a simple formula, the strategies to accomplish these four things take a little more doing. So we're going to look at each of them individually.

I SEE IT—GAIN THEIR ATTENTION

The numbers are all over the place in terms of how long you have to capture and maintain someone's attention, but suffice to say you don't have much time at all. Like, less than three seconds to capture their attention and less than fifteen to keep them engaged. (If you're doing public speaking, you've got around seven seconds to grab 'em before you lose 'em. No pressure, right?)

Even crazier, as technology grows more popular and pervasive, the shorter our attention spans have become. We're at a point now where even goldfish have longer attention spans than we do![47]

So when it comes to marketing your business, learning how to capture attention is a game you'll have to learn to play.

---

[47] Kevin McSpadden, "You Now Have A Shorter Attention Span Than A Goldfish," *Time*, May 14, 2015, https://time.com/3858309/attention-spans-goldfish.

And there are three keys to playing it well:

- Attraction
- Disruption
- Alignment

If you want to be a ninja at capturing people's attention, you've got to *attract* them to something pleasing, *disrupt* them with something that sparks their curiosity, or *align* with them to something they already believe and feel.

When it comes to *attraction*, you want your marketing piece to be positioned in such a way that someone likes it—it's pleasing to the eye. Think of how clothing stores utilize professional models for marketing. They slap their outfits on an attractive person … and it makes you want to buy.

But have you noticed how models don't look like they used to, all air-brushed, thin, and perfect? That's because our culture now sees *authenticity* as more attractive than perfection. If you don't take notice of changes like this, you'll miss it in the marketplace.

So when it comes to attracting potential customers, be genuine. Don't try to make things seem perfect. Just be real. If you've given some thought as to who your target customer is, you know them better than anyone else, so think about what would attract them.

The second way to gain someone's attention is through *disruption*.

Did you know one of the best-selling print magazines of all time is the *National Enquirer*? Yeah, that one. Everyone knows most of the stories are fake. But the editors of this magazine have mastered the art of the disruptive headline, and it moves their product fast.

You're standing in the checkout line at the grocery store, waiting there with nothing to do. Then you look over and see a headline that completely disrupts your train of thought. "Pope Francis wants to get married!"

Instantly, you think to yourself, *Wait, I didn't think the Pope could get married.* You know deep down it's not true, but everything in you wants to see what it's all about. Since you don't have time to read it in the aisle, you buy it. The next thing you know, you're reading it in the car (not speaking from experience here, of course!).

That's the power of disruption. And while we've never purchased that magazine in our lives, a simple Google search for "*National Enquirer* headlines" will help spark your inner disruptor. The publisher has mastered the art of getting your attention via disruption.

Expert Owners never tell lies to get attention, but disruptive marketing is good in many ways. Think of a headline like this: "Gain more muscle without working out!" (You're in, right?) Just keep in mind—people may like disruption, but they do *not* like being shocked. So don't go overboard.

The third way to attract a customer is through *alignment*. This is when you and your customer share the same values, and your marketing highlights that commonality. When *your* why lines up with *their* why, they are likely to buy.

We saw this play out in our business just after we were fired by HGTV. After our faces were plastered all over the news, we found even more Christians wanting to use our company to buy or sell a house. We also received phone calls from other agents who were believers and wanted to purchase a franchise—all because their values aligned with ours.

After you've gained someone's attention, you then need to arouse their interest. Capturing attention is great, but it isn't enough. You've got to get them moving in your direction.

I LIKE IT—PIQUE THEIR INTEREST

We've found that one of the most powerful ways to gain someone's interest is through a question and a statement. You start with a question they would say "yes" to, then follow it with a "How To / Without" statement. We first learned this from Russell Brunson, and it's been super helpful to us.

See if this arouses your interest:

"Do you want to lose your belly fat?"

You're probably nodding your head right now. *(Jason: I know David is.)* Okay, now to the statement that invites curiosity:

"We're going to show you HOW TO lose your belly fat WITHOUT giving up your favorite foods."

Does that make you want to learn more? Of course, it does. It doesn't matter if you're grossly overweight or shredded out of your mind; a statement like that makes you want to find out how it works.

The reason why is because a "How To / Without" statement has a little psychology behind it. When you craft the statement, you're actually targeting two very specific things—a person's desire and their pain.

The "how to" touches on their current desire. The "without" touches on the fear or pain that has kept them from achieving their desire. It looks like this:

How to (achieve your desire) without (experiencing pain).[48]

Do you remember the chapter on branding where we

---

[48] Russell Brunson, *Expert Secrets.*

discussed the importance of targeting both external and internal desires? It's the same thing here. Your "how to" statement hits their *external* desire and your "without" statement hits their *internal* desire. However, in this situation you're specifically targeting their *internal* fear or pain.

If you can help someone get what they want while alleviating their fear or pain, you will certainly pique their interest. How to lose belly fat is the desire of a *lot* of people. But they don't want to go through the pain of actually doing it. Or they fear that they'll start but won't be able to finish. Your *How To / Without* statement stirs up their interest because it relieves them of this pressure.

Here are a few examples:

"Do you want to build a successful business?" Heads start nodding. "I'm going to show you *how to* crush it in business *without* sacrificing the relationships you value most."

"Do you want green grass?" Yes! "Here's *how to* get it *without* hiring an overpriced landscaper."

"Have you ever had a business deal go south?" Of course. "Here's *how to* unwind a deal gone wrong *without* jumping off a bridge or hiring a hitman." (Believe it or not, we actually have a course coming out on this in the future, which talks about forgiveness in the context of work.)[49]

The possibilities are endless, so have fun with it.

Grabbing someone's attention and gaining their interest happens in an instant—all within seconds. Once you've got them moving in your direction, it's time for the third phase of marketing: *desire*.

---

[49] Go to BenhamBrothers.com for more information on our courses.

I WANT IT—AROUSE THEIR DESIRE

Have you ever seen the movie *Napoleon Dynamite?* Uncle Rico is selling Tupperware to an older couple, and to seal the deal he throws in a completely random little boat in a bottle, like the ones you see at a beach store. The older woman looks down at it with longing eyes and says to her husband, "I want that!"

That's the goal of your marketing. When you've captured their attention and gained their interest you want to get them to say exactly what this woman said—"I want that!" (Though Uncle Rico's boat was ridiculous!)

Over the years, we've discovered one of the most powerful ways to create desire in someone for your product or service is to use your STORY. *The New York Times* once described marketing as "the art of telling stories so enthralling that people lose track of their wallets."[50]

We cannot overemphasize how truly powerful stories are in marketing. Our brains are wired for story. The reason we like stories so much is that we get to experience things without having to actually go through them.

It's what happens when you watch a movie, and you begin to feel the same emotions of the characters. If you're anything like our wives, you bawl through every romance movie you watch (*Jason: I've seen David scream cry a time or two*). That's because the emotional part of your brain can't tell if you're the one going through the situation or if it's someone else.[51]

---

[50] Charles Duhigg, "Why Don't You Donate for Syrian Refugees? Blame Bad Marketing," *The New York Times*, June 14, 2017, https://www.nytimes.com/2017/06/14/business/media/marketing-charity-water-syria.html.
[51] Lisa Cron, *Wired for Story: The Writer's Guide to Using Brain Science to Hook Readers from the Very First Sentence* (Ten Speed Press, 2012).

The use of story allows people to feel a connection to you, which makes them want to buy from you. And when it comes to arousing desire in others for your product or service, the best story to use is your own.

Don't tell yourself you don't have a good story—everyone does. Your story doesn't need to be glamorous or epic. It just needs one key critical component: your "Aha!" moment. That moment where you were at the end of your rope, then you discovered something amazing, and you're now able to help others in the same way you helped yourself.

Maybe it sounds something like this:

"I always struggled to lose the tire around my waist. Every time I'd start a new diet in January, I was crushing ice cream and Ho Hos by Valentine's Day. Nothing worked. Until I discovered _____. All of a sudden, I was eating many of my favorite foods while shedding weight fast. So, I recorded everything I did, broke it down into six simple steps, and now I'm going to share it with you."

There was nothing glamorous about that story, but it hits home with lots of people. It gets them saying, "I want what you have."

The other day, I (Jason) was in a TJ Maxx following my wife around when I found myself in the aisle with all the rare foods you don't typically see at the grocery store. I picked up two different bags of coffee, both of which looked amazing. I looked at the labels on the back. One of them described how good the coffee was. The other had a picture of a family and a small story of how and why they started their business. The one with the story connected with me immediately, and before I knew it, I had tossed it in the cart and put the other one back on the shelf.

That's the power of story. Have you heard the phrase, "People buy on emotion but justify on logic?" Well, it's true. And there's no better way to engage the emotions of people than through a story.

There are a few rules of thumb when it comes to using your story in marketing, specifically with how you want to share it and what needs to be included in it.

First, when you share your story, it needs to be:

- Relatable
- Vulnerable
- Bold

You don't need to have all three in every story. But you need at least one in order to arouse their desire.

You want to be *relatable*: "I was in the same spot you are." This is why having an epic story sometimes misses people, because they can't relate. Using your everyday experiences, just like everyone else has, is easier to relate to.

You also need to be *vulnerable.* Share your flaws. Don't position yourself as perfect. Let people know how you messed up but what you did to fix it. People are drawn to vulnerability.

When we give our talk on standing boldly for what you believe in, we tell people that the secret to courage is first recognizing your inner coward. Then we share a time in our lives when we nearly caved to the pressure to stay quiet about our beliefs because we were scared. With heads nodding all around, we then share how God gives us courage *through* the fear and not away from it. It hits home, because everyone knows what it means to be afraid.

Lastly, be **_BOLD_**. Like a word in all caps, bolded, underlined, and italicized. It stands out!

People are turned off by boring and neutral. They want someone who's bold, funny, different, and decisive. Use polarity in your story, otherwise you'll blend in with the rest, and the only desire people will have is to buy someone else's product or service. That's what happened in TJ Maxx with that bag of coffee I put back on the shelf. It was just another boring marketing piece about how good their product was.

Okay, that's *how* you share your story. Next, let's look at *what* you should include in it.

Your story needs to answer these three key questions:

- What makes you unique?
- What is your proven process?
- What is your guarantee?

What makes you unique? In the branding phase, we talked about how God has made you unique and He wants to use your uniqueness to bless the world. Well, when sharing your story, tell people what makes you different from the rest.

Gino Wickman, in his bestselling business book *Traction*, encourages entrepreneurs to list out their "three uniques" when crafting their marketing plans.[52] Southwest Airlines lists their three as 1) low fares, 2) on time flights, 3) having fun. If you've seen a Southwest commercial, you'll see these three playing themselves out in all their marketing.

Next, what is your proven process? In the example earlier, we mentioned the six-step process for trimming your belly fat. People geek out over proven processes. Why? Because if someone else did it, they can do it too. And if the process is simple enough, all they have to do is follow the steps and they'll get results.

---

[52] Gino Wickman, *Traction: Get a Grip on Your Business* (BenBella Books, 2012).

The book you hold in your hands is our proven twelve-step process that can help you move through the four cycles of entrepreneurship—from a wannapreneur to a solopreneur to an entrepreneur and ultimately to a SeeYaPreneur. You're reading it now because you *desire* to know more and find the same success.

Last, what is your guarantee? What is the promise you deliver? For our Expert Ownership course, we promise to show you how to serve God, thrive in business, and live a life of impact ... without sacrificing what's most important. And if you take the course and aren't happy with it, then we'll give you a full refund. A guarantee elicits confidence in the buyer; they know you can be trusted.

When you've got people wanting what you have by leveraging the power of your story, it's time to move them to the fourth phase of your marketing—*action!* This is the best part, because the minute people start buying, you're in business!

I'LL BUY IT—MOVE THEM TO ACTION

This step is your sales. When your marketing is really good, sales will come naturally, and you won't see a gap between the two. (We'll break down sales further in the next chapter. For now, let's stick with marketing.)

There are four key components that move people to action:

- Scarcity
- Urgency
- Clarity
- Simplicity

Let's look at each of these through a lens many of us are familiar with—shopping on Amazon.

First, *scarcity*. When you find what you want, but you see a little red line that says, "Only 2 left—order soon." Scarcity plays on FOMO (fear of missing out), which is the greatest fear buyers have. Research shows that the fear of loss is greater than the desire for gain.[53] Amazon uses scarcity brilliantly.

Then there's *urgency*. The fact Amazon shows only a few more left already gives you a sense of urgency, but when they put, "Get this item by tomorrow," they are enlivening your sense of urgency so you will act fast.

Next is *clarity*. This is where you clear the path to purchase by removing obstacles standing in the way. One of the best ways to do this is through customer reviews. Before you buy anything on Amazon, what do you do? You check the reviews, because you want to know you're buying the right thing. Those reviews remove the obstacles in your mind because other people felt what you feel and let you see the result of their decision.

And finally, when it comes to moving someone to action, you need *simplicity*. This is what we call the "Amazon effect." It is so incredibly simple to buy from them that when you find a product anywhere else, what do you typically do? Check Amazon first to see if you can get it there. This is the reason Best Buy is closing many of its stores—they've become a glorified showroom where people look at the product, only to order it on Amazon.

Amazon even has this awesome "Buy It Now" button where you don't have to do anything other than swipe right and the product will be on your doorstep in twenty-four hours. (How did people survive fifty years ago?)

It really isn't fair, but this is the world we live in. So, learn

---

[53] D.Kahneman and A. Tversky, "Prospect theory: An analysis of decision under risk," *Econometrica*, 47, 263-291, 1979.

to leverage the clever use of scarcity, urgency, clarity, and simplicity. This will move people to action. When you adopt this technique, you'll realize the blessing good ol' Elias St. Elmo Lewis brought us so many years ago when he developed the AIDA marketing model.

- Attention
- Interest
- Desire
- Action

That's the goal of your marketing.

But there's one key component many people add at the end: *retention*. It's easier to keep an existing customer than to get a new one. Some companies call this "Closing the Back Door." You do such a good job with your service that they want to keep buying from you. (We'll talk about that in the chapter on Value Delivery.)

Everyone wants to buy. Nobody wants to be sold.

If you utilize the AIDA model in your marketing, you will find your small business might not be so small anymore. You will be well on your way to crushing it as an Expert Owner.

If you want to dive deeper into understanding and implementing marketing strategies and tactics, add our online course *Expert Ownership: Mastering Marketing* to your list of to-dos. It's a course designed to build on the principles we covered in this chapter and more.

Your marketing is the setup for your sales process. It's one thing to capture people's eyeballs, but it's another matter altogether to convert them to customers. And, fortunately for us, we discovered nine traits that helped us do just that.

SALES

SeeYaPreneur

↗ 12. Money

/ 11. Leadership

/ 10. Team Building

/ 09. Systems

/ 08. Value Delivery

/ **07. Sales**

/ 06. Marketing

/ 05. Value Creation

/ 04. Branding

/ 03. Ideation

/ 02. Core Four

/ 01. Identity

CHAPTER SIXTEEN

SALES:
CONVERT YOUR PROSPECTS

You've captured leads through your marketing. Now it's time to close those deals and make sales. While marketing is the art of gaining prospects, sales is the art of converting those prospects into purchasers. It's getting them to say "yes" and be happy about their decision. Because (and say it with us) *everyone wants to buy, but nobody wants to be sold.*

Do you know what will make you good at sales? When your customer never feels like you're trying to sell them anything. Instead, they feel like you have their best interests in mind. Why? Because an Expert Owner really does have their best interests in mind.

The last thing you want is to become some pesky salesperson who manipulates people into buying something they don't need. The best businesses operate by motivation, not manipulation. As our friend John Maxwell says, "Manipulation is about MY benefit. Motivation is about MUTUAL benefit."[54]

Expert Owners always seek mutual benefit, which is why we talk so much about making an impact with your income—the kind of impact that honors God, strengthens relationships, and builds families.

But there are plenty of entrepreneurs out there who don't think this way. For instance, the makers of Grand Theft

---

[54] Leadership guru John Maxwell teaches this concept throughout his books.

Autohave built a small empire around a video game that glorifies shooting police officers and legitimizes rape. They're leveraging the power of branding, marketing, and sales, but only to manipulate people into buying something that destroys them mentally, emotionally, and spiritually.

They sell a lot of that product and make a ton of money. But what does that matter in the eternal scheme of things? Shame on them. That's not the path for you.

An Expert Owner starts with a product or service that can solve a problem AND is good for the people who buy it. When you have a solution like that, it's your responsibility to make a clear path for people to get it. That's where the act of sales comes in.

The problem for many entrepreneurs who aren't salespeople by nature is that they love it when people buy ... but they hate having to sell. We know the feeling. But the point of this chapter is that the best salespeople aren't those who try to convince you to buy anything. They simply present you with what you need, remove any obstacles in the way, and lead you through the process until your needs are met.

When you do this, you are no longer considered a "salesperson" but a "problem solver."

And we're about to show you how to approach your sales this way: becoming a problem solver who excels at converting prospects into purchasers without needing to "convince" anyone to buy anything.

In our first business, we had to sell both a service *and* a product. We were always on the lookout for clients who could use our service (banks needing to sell foreclosed houses) and customers who would buy our product (buyers looking to purchase a house). *Clients* used our service and *customers* bought our product.

Not everyone has to sell products *and* services. But because we did, the experience gave us an incredible, well-rounded education on the art of closing deals. Looking back on how we were able to gain more than two hundred bank clients and sell houses to more than thirty-two thousand customers, the one thing we attribute our success to most was our *approach* to sales.

No system or strategy can do for you what the right approach will do.

Your approach is the mindset you bring to the sales process. It's what gives you the power to close *any deal* to *anyone* at *any time*.

Too many entrepreneurs fail in business because they focus more on sales systems and strategies than their approach to selling. We don't want you to make that mistake. So we're going to spend the rest of this chapter talking about what we found to be the most valuable aspect of sales—our *approach*.

Using baseball once again as an analogy, anyone who knows the game knows that the best hitters are the ones who have the best approach. A hitter's approach is all the stuff that goes on in his head before he swings the bat. It's his confidence, his self-control, his desire to have fun, how loose he is, his ability to laser focus, etc. Whatever goes on in between his ears is what defines his approach.

Show us a hitter who's distracted by off-the-field stuff, lacks confidence because he's in a slump, can't stop swinging at bad pitches, doesn't think the game is fun anymore, has lost his ability to focus, or is completely uptight, and we'll show you a hitter who will fail almost every single time he steps up to the plate. Why? His approach is off.

Being good at sales starts with your mindset for sales. The best agents we had in our real estate company were *those who never really tried to sell anything.* Honestly! Their mindset was to simply serve others, so they focused on helping people find the house that fit their family in a neighborhood they loved at a price they could afford. Earning a commission was icing on the cake.

Our top agent was my (Jason's) brother-in-law, Frankie Cantadore. He was a former college athlete who joined our firm shortly after college and spent a decade selling houses for us. In that time, he sold more homes than any other agent we had ... by far.

His secret? Food. Think "Guy Fieri" from the reality TV show *Diners, Drive-ins, and Dives,* and you'll start to understand his excitement for fine cuisine.

Selling real estate was a front for his true passion, "professional" taste-testing! The minute a prospective homebuyer called he'd light up like a Christmas tree at the opportunity to tell them of all the little *foodie* joints in town— offering to meet at one of his favorite spots. Thirty days and several hole-in-the-wall visits later, they were closing a deal.

While Frankie wasn't aware of what he was doing, we could see it. He never once *tried* to sell a house. He just knew that people need food as badly as they need a place to live. And since most people "love" food, he figured he'd meet that need first. Helping them curb their physical appetite with some amazing dishes actually stirred up their transactional appetite to work with him.

When you keep your customers' needs and wants at the core, then everything else will fall into place. You move away from a mindset of "I'm here to CONVINCE you," to one of "I'm here to HELP you." And people can tell the difference.

Granted, none of us would be in business in the first place if there wasn't the hope of making money. We get that. Human beings are wired for reward, and there's nothing wrong with that. In fact, God made us that way.

But when you choose a field of endeavor and you begin working with customers, while money may have been your motivator to get you into that line of work, it should never be your motivator while working with a customer or client. Helping them get what they need—that must be your motivator. Seeing the smiles on their faces and the satisfaction in their eyes—that's what should compel you.

When you approach your work like that, then sales will chase you down.

We saw this mindset work brilliantly a few years into our business when we got a phone call from a prospective client we'd been trying to land for a long time. We had prayed for over a year for this bank to bite, but they never called us back.

Then one day, out of the blue, they called.

I (David) remember when Jason took the phone call. He got up and started pacing as he talked. Then he got quiet. I knew the asset manager on the other line was probably questioning why she should hire a couple of newbie brokers who didn't have the same experience as other seasoned agents.

Then Jason spoke up. "Ma'am," he said, "if you're looking to hire agents who have more experience than us, that's okay. I get it. But if you want to hire two of the hungriest guys you'll ever meet who will stop at nothing to exceed your expectations, remove your headache, and make it their primary aim to get you promoted, then we're your guys!"

When he hung up the phone, he looked at me and said, "I think we got 'em!" I wanted to hug him (but I refrained because we don't really do that sort of thing).

I (Jason) remember the feeling when I hung up the phone. Even though she didn't hire us on the spot, I could tell she'd liked what she'd heard. The feeling was better than when I hit my first home run as an Oriole in the Minor Leagues. As fun as it was to touch all the bases that night, it was nothing compared to the feeling of converting a prospect into a purchaser. All we needed was for her to call us back and make it official.

But the truth is, I wasn't trying to *sell* anything that day. My goal was to make her aware that we had systematized and streamlined our business to a point where hiring us would make her job much easier. If I just made that clear, then she could make an informed decision. When I mentioned our goal to get her promoted, I could hear the energy in her voice as she responded. She liked it ... a lot.

Although I didn't realize it at the time, when I assured her that we could sell her houses AND get her promoted, I was speaking to both her external need and her internal desire. Of course, she wasn't consciously thinking about getting promoted when she called me, but I was. And when I made her aware of it, it made an impact.

But before I tell you if she called back, you need to know two things about that call that are uber-important.

First, a few days after the call, I had to meet a homeowner at his house to negotiate a deal for a bank. He had missed more than a year's worth of payments, so they needed him to sign a few documents. I was in a hurry that day because I had a ton of stuff to do, so I planned on delivering the paperwork and jetting out in less than ten minutes. But when he started opening up about his personal and family issues, I felt God prompting me to stay and talk.

Tears streamed down his cheeks as we chatted. We sat on his front porch for well over an hour. Then he stood up, gave me a massive bear hug, and thanked me for listening to him.

When I got back in the car, I saw I had missed several calls from David. By the time I got in touch with him, he couldn't hold back his excitement. "Dude!" he said. "I've been trying to call you. I just got an email from that asset manager you talked to a few days ago. She officially hired us!"

At that moment, I felt such a peace and joy come over me. It was as if God said, "See, if you focus on *My* thing, I'll take care of *your* thing." I didn't want to spend an hour with that man that morning—I was in a hurry. But when God prompted me to listen to the heart of a broken man, He was behind the scenes prompting the heart of an asset manager to hire us! It was a humbling experience.

God isn't looking for your flashy sales strategy; He's looking for your faithfulness. And when you're faithful, He'll open doors that can't be opened any other way.

The second thing you need to know about that phone call is that my heart's desire *really was* to get her promoted. Those weren't just words I said to close a deal. The more time I spent praying about landing that client, the more I felt God encouraging me to be concerned with her as a person rather than just interested in doing business with her. That's when I started to think about what she truly wanted that went deeper than just selling houses. God was directing me before I even knew about all this *internal / external* need stuff.

Like we said earlier, that's the power of partnering with God in your business. He will lead you to do the right thing even if you don't know what that thing should be.

NINE PILLARS

So let's get practical here. When we look back at that phone call, there were nine key qualities at work that helped us convert the asset manager from a prospect to a purchaser. We call them *pillars* because pillars are both structural and ornamental; they hold up a solid amount of weight and they look good doing it.

The weight of your entire sales process rests on these nine pillars, and when you apply them to your interaction with prospects, your business will not only look good, but will be standing on a firm foundation. They not only work for in-person sales, but are true for online and physical ads, sales copy, videos, funnels, and whatever else you use in your business.

Here they are:

1. *Be Personable.* This pillar acts as the foundation for all the others. When selling your product or service, you are dealing with real people. Your job is to manage those relationships. And the best way to do that is to change the way you see the people with whom you are making transactions. You need to genuinely care for them. Base your sales process on the following statement:

The path to Expert Ownership is paved by creating friendships more than closing prospects.

How you *see* people determines how you *treat* people. If you see your prospects more as future friends than future customers, you'll treat them as such.

If you see them as simply prospects, then your desire for friendship will be replaced by a thirst for finances. They will see right through you and have a hard time trusting you. But if you see them as a friend, then you're going to be genuinely concerned with who they are as a person. You won't have to *try* to care for them because it will come from the heart. They will know it, and they will trust you because of it.

As we said in earlier chapters, being good at business is being good at relationships. When it comes to sales, consider yourself to be in the relationship-building business. It will go a long way in drawing people into your business ecosystem.

2. *Be Purposeful.* One of the best things you can do in sales is to fully understand your prospect's WHY. You not only need to know why they are interested in and need your product, but also why they care in the first place. Remember: When your WHY lines up with their WHY, they will buy.

We saw this play out in the phone call with that asset manager. Her WHY for being an employee of the bank was to earn a living for her family. Obviously, getting promoted would help her with that goal. When I mentioned that I would make it my goal to help her get promoted, my WHY lined up with her WHY. The result was a closed sale.

Another powerful aspect of being purposeful is sharing your story, just like you do in branding and marketing. Let them know who you are and why you do what you do—both as a person and as a company. This helps to align their desires with your desires; they realize that you are just like them and that you want what they want.

3. *Be Powerful.* Walk in confidence! Nobody will buy from someone unsure of themselves or the solution they have. You need to be fully convinced in your mind that what you're selling is what people need, and that you are the person for the job! Period. End of discussion.

When I (Jason) had that surge of adrenaline that day on the phone call with the asset manager, I could tell she was drawn to my confidence in what we could do to help her. But I remember a time a few years earlier when I wasn't so confident in what I was selling.

A buddy of ours asked us to help him sell little electronic massagers at a trade conference. And because we were flat broke, we said we'd do it. The first person I talked to asked me more questions than I could answer. The more he talked, the more exhausted I became, to the point where I walked over and sat in a chair and watched David try and fail over and over again.

I had zero confidence, and therefore zero ability to sell anything. *(David: I had plenty of confidence, but the product was junk—so that was that.)*

Your job in sales is to lead. You need to confidently lead the person to the solution they need. People come to you because they have a problem, and they don't know what to do about it. So lead with confidence!

4. *Be Passionate.* I (David) saw Jason lose his passion that day at the trade conference when he sat against the wall and gave up. It was like he'd turned into a little kid who'd received a remote-control car for Christmas, only to discover it didn't work. He sat there with the thing in his hand like, "This is so stupid ... I hate being here."

Passion acts like a magnet. Our dad used to say, "The greatest orator is the person who's in love with their message." It doesn't matter what the message is; if you're passionate about it, people will be interested.

An entrepreneur's passion tends to simmer when their focus is more on selling a product than helping a person. Or when they're so busy trying to keep the business afloat they don't have the time to enjoy the process of solving people's problems.

Don't let either of these be true about you. Be zealous about how you can help others ... and watch as they flock to you.

5. *Be Persuasive.* The most persuasive people are not those who try to convince you of something, but those who live the life they promote or use the product they are trying to sell. Have you ever seen an overweight fitness instructor? We've seen a few, and there's nothing persuasive that makes us want to hire them as a coach.

The power of your own life story is incredibly persuasive, as are the stories of others. Testimonies of how your product or service helped another person can go a long way toward closing a deal. By the way, we've found one of the best opportunities to use other people's stories is when *objections* enter the picture. When that happens, we've found a three-step process works wonders:

- Feel: "I know what you're feeling ..."
- Felt: "I felt the same way ..."
- Found: "But here's what I found ..."[55]

"I know what you're feeling. John felt the same way, but here's what he found ..."

When people know that others have used your product or service successfully, it's extremely persuasive.

6. *Be Proactive.* When it comes to landing a sale, most experts agree that it takes somewhere between seven and thirteen "touches" before a person will choose

---

[55] Myra Golden, MyraGolden.com/blog

to buy.[56] Being proactive is all about making contact regularly and not giving up.

The key is to make prospecting part of your daily routine. Reach out consistently. Our goal was to reach out to twenty asset managers a day. We did that for ten years. At the end of a decade, we had more than two hundred clients, each one representing tens of thousands and some even millions of dollars in revenue.

This is where the tripod of wealth comes into play that we discussed back in Chapter Ten. When you're disciplined, diligent, and determined, you'll be proactive to close the deal.

7. *Be Patient.* We all know that patience is a virtue. But when it comes to sales, patience is more than a virtue … it's sanity! If you're not patient, you'll go crazy (and you'll drive your prospects mad as well). Both of you lose in that scenario.

You can't be pushy with people. Not only will this turn them off, but it will also send you on a downward spiral. Your stress levels will go through the roof because you won't be able to understand why the person isn't as excited about your product or service as you are.

Remember, you're in it for the long haul. Just be patient. Let customers come to the decision on their own, not because you pushed them into making a quick decision. Then, if they happen to have a bad experience, they won't blame you for it— they'll know the decision was theirs alone. Yeah, they might be upset, and you'll need to make things right … but they won't write you off. They might give you another shot.

---

[56] Laurie Beasley, "Why It Takes 7 to 13+ Touches to Deliver a Qualified Sales Lead (Part 1), Online Marketing Institute, Oct. 10, 2013, https://www. onlinemarketinginstitute.org/blog/2013/10/why-it-takes-7-to-13-touches-to-deliver-a-qualified-sales-lead-part1/

So trust God and let patience work in your heart and in the heart of your prospective customer.

8. *Be Principled.* There's no use selling something that isn't good for the person. You may make money, but you haven't done them any favors.

Being a principled salesperson is about establishing proper boundaries and refusing to go outside of those boundaries just to make a buck.

An Expert Owner has no desire to profit from doing business with a company that makes video games where people are rewarded for committing crime. They refuse to coach a business owner who produces pornography or promotes activities that would harm people and relationships. It doesn't matter how much money is at stake in these situations; if you're operating by principles, you'll walk away every time.

Being principled is not just about avoiding bad things; it's also refusing to sell a good thing at the wrong time. Maybe the person can't afford it right now and should wait. Maybe they have too much debt and would only incur further debt by purchasing your product. Having the fortitude to say, "You know what, now may not be the best time for you to buy … let's revisit in six months," puts you on the path to God's blessing over your sales.

9. *Be Pleasant.* Have fun! Have a good time when you're telling people about your product or service. A smile is attractive. Creating humorous memes and ad slicks or entertaining sales copy lightens the mood and sets people at ease. It will make your job not only easier but much more enjoyable.

If you're not having a good time with the people you interact with in your line of business, then you won't have the energy to stay motivated. Relax a bit, loosen that tie, and have a little fun!

In closing, if these nine character qualities guide your sales efforts, you will find yourself not only increasing your finances but also your friendships. (And what could be better than having your new friends pay you!?)

So, that's it for marketing and sales.

Your marketing generates prospects.

Your sales converts those prospects into purchasers.

Now it's time to move them to the final phase in our three-phase upcycle—the best one of all—turning your purchasers into promoters. We're about to show you the one key you'll need to do just that.

STEP EIGHT

VALUE DELIVERY

SeeYaPreneur

↗ 12. Money

/ 11. Leadership

/ 10. Team Building

/ 09. Systems

/ **08. Value Delivery**

/ 07. Sales

/ 06. Marketing

/ 05. Value Creation

/ 04. Branding

/ 03. Ideation

/ 02. Core Four

/ 01. Identity

CHAPTER SEVENTEEN

VALUE DELIVERY:
DELIVER YOUR PRODUCT

No matter what your business provides, value delivery is where the rubber meets the road. This is when you *deliver* what you promised and prove to the customer you can be trusted to meet his or her need.

Your business is a value delivery system. It involves everything you do to make sure a paying customer is a happy customer: order processing, inventory management, delivery/fulfillment, troubleshooting, customer service, etc. Without value delivery, you don't have business.[57]

Superior value delivery is what separates the champs from the chumps. Or, if you're sensitive to that type of lingo, it's what separates the businesses that make it from those that don't.

Most importantly, the value delivery phase gives you the opportunity to reach the highest level of the three-phase upcycle and turn your *purchasers* into *promoters*. When your business delivers with excellence and serves well, your customers will subconsciously join your sales and marketing team (without adding a single penny to your expense column)!

But if you fail to deliver on your promises, then those purchasers will turn to pessimists instead of promoters. They'll not only refuse to buy from you again but make sure others don't as well. We all know how damaging a bad review can be.

---

[57] Josh Kaufman, *The Personal MBA: Master the Art of Business* (Portfolio, 2012).

Even worse, if your customer knows you're a person of faith and you fail to deliver, they might even question the God you worship. And nothing—we repeat, NOTHING—is worse than making God look bad. Our work is meant to be our primary form of worship. We call it *worKship*. The way we work should reflect the truth of God; and everything God does is good.[58]

This is why value delivery is such an important part of your business: It's your opportunity to bring God glory by serving people with excellence. And to top it off, you can earn a decent living at the same time.

You can have the best branding, marketing, and sales in the world, but the real value of the Expert Owner is not in what is *promised*. It's in what is *delivered*.

Here's the key—people don't just buy your product or service; they buy an *experience* with it.

Imagine that you go to the dentist to get a cavity filled, but the experience goes something like this: The Lidocaine doesn't work and one of the dentist's drills breaks halfway through the process. You'd never go back, right? Even if he ultimately gets the job done, you didn't pay to simply have a cavity filled. You paid to have a good experience (or at least not a horrifying one!) while having a hole drilled into your tooth and filled back in.

You walk into a dentist's office with a certain set of expectations. But if your experience doesn't line up with your expectations, the dentist loses you as a customer. Because of bad service, he turns you from promoter to pessimist.

Maya Angelou once said, "I've learned that people will forget

---

[58] We teach the *WorKship* concept in our membership @ ExpertOwnership. com.

what you said, people will forget what you did, but they will never forget how you made them feel."[59] This quote captures the heart of excellent value delivery in business.

People purchase because of *expectation*. But they promote because of *experience*.

In order for people to buy, expectation has to be high. Your marketing and sales set that expectation. We've already discussed this.

But for people to promote, you must *exceed* their expectation.

If you *meet* their expectation, they'll be happy and will probably buy from you again. But if you *exceed* their expectation, they'll not only be happy and want to do business with you again … they'll make sure others do the same. They'll move from purchaser to promoter, and you will have earned yourself a new best friend.

This one principle revolutionized our business and set us so far ahead of our competition that they couldn't keep up. We encapsulated it in one of our core principles, which we shared earlier:

Give more in value than you take in pay.

Jesus is the one who first taught this lesson. In His time, Roman law required a Jew to carry a Roman soldier's gear for up to a mile if commanded to do so. Jesus flipped that paradigm when He taught His fellow Jews, "If a soldier demands that you carry his gear for a mile, carry it two miles" (Matthew 5:41).

---

[59] Maya Angelou, "People Will Never Forget How You Made Them Feel," Self Improvement Daily, Aug. 27, 2020, https://www.selfimprovementdailytips. com/podcast/people-will-never-forget-how-you-made-them-feel-maya-angelou.

The first mile was out of obligation, but the second mile was out of love. This is one of the reasons Christianity spread like wildfire throughout the Roman Empire. Going the second mile opened the hearts of people to hear about the faith of those who would do such a thing. And it unlocked supernatural power in the early church.

You can easily do the same, right in your place of business. When you give more in value than you take in pay, it will endear you in the hearts of your customers. They'll be open to hear more about why you serve the way you do. They'll also feel loyal to you and will want to see you succeed. And as we said in the chapter on sales, they'll become your friends.

BE THE BUSBOY

Operating by a "second-mile mindset" was etched in our memories as young boys when our dad took us to a Denny's restaurant in Dallas, Texas. We were pretty jazzed about smashing some pancakes, until Dad told us we weren't there to eat but to watch someone work. Talk about an unmet expectation.

When we arrived, there was a large group of people huddled around a big window. Intrigued, we made our way over and joined them.

"Just watch the busboy," Dad said to us. "Do you see him? The older man in his fifties with the white apron and hat?"

We peered through the window and saw a man walking slowly, pushing a cart down the aisle. When he came to a dirty, vacant table, he stopped the cart and analyzed the scene. He looked at his watch, looked back at the table ... then, BOOM!

For the next twenty seconds, he painted one of the most incredible pictures of work ethic we've ever seen. It was like something out of a cartoon. Dishes went flying into one bucket, utensils into another, trash in the bag; he whipped out a washcloth to clean every inch of the table and chairs, and then perfectly stationed the salt, pepper, and sugar on a now-immaculate table. Everything was put in the proper place for the next patrons.

Now we understood why so many people stood outside the windows—they were there to see the busboy! When he finished the table, those watching him erupted in applause. But he just calmly looked back at his watch with a clear expression of satisfaction on his face, and quietly strolled to the next table.

Dad looked over at us and said, "Every job is sacred. Every job is worthy of your best effort. It doesn't matter what the job is. You make it the best you can and turn it into something people are cheering about because your effort inspires them."

We didn't get to eat those famous Denny's pancakes that day, but the busboy showed us the power of doing more than you're paid to do. This man was paid to simply clean tables, but he turned his job into an experience for those in the restaurant. As a result, that place consistently had a line out the door of people waiting to watch him work.

He gave more in value than he took in pay. He exceeded the expectations not only of his employer, but of every customer who stepped foot in that restaurant. And because of it, we're still talking about him more than thirty years later.

STACK IT UP

We had an opportunity to put this principle into practice at the very beginning of our business. As with any new endeavor, our early years were pretty lean financially. To offset our lack of income, we took any odd jobs we could get our hands on.

Fortunately, we had friends who had friends.

One of them was the owner of a printing company who needed a day's worth of work. He could pay us $8 an hour. It wasn't the highest we've ever been paid, but it was something.

When we arrived in the morning for the day of work, the manager escorted the two of us to the back of the warehouse. It was a huge facility with several printers and about ten workers stacking paper on pallets.

He led us to three large pallets and said, "All right, boys. I wish I had full-time work for you, but I don't. All I need for you to do is take these and restack them in reverse order. They got out of whack with our printer, so I need you guys to fix it."

He told us it would take about eight hours to complete and that he would come back at the end of the day.

With our newfound temporary boss gone, we got to work. Four hours later, the job was done. That left us with four more hours. We had a choice: kick back and let the clock tick away … or do more than he expected us to do. Although we didn't know the term at the time, it was a value delivery choice.

We remembered the busboy. So we started looking around the warehouse. The entire back section was disorganized. There were boxes everywhere and wrapping paper all over the place. It looked like a tornado had just hit the place.

We decided to spend the rest of our time making sense of all that mess. So the two of us got to work. By the time the manager came back, it was fully cleaned and put in order.

We'll never forget the look on his face when he walked in. He browsed the warehouse with his mouth gaped open. "Who did this?" he asked.

"We did," we replied.

"I want to hire you both full-time!" he said.

We learned in that moment that when you give more in value than you take in pay, doors that were once closed suddenly open. He didn't have full-time positions when he hired us, but when we exceeded his expectation, full-time jobs magically opened up.

That owner went from a *prospect* (a person with a need looking for a solution) to a *purchaser* (he hired us to do a day's worth of work) to a *promoter* (he wanted to promote us to full-time employees).

Of course, this is a different play on the word *promoter*. If you're an employee, exceeding expectations will get you a promotion; you'll move up the ladder. But if you're an entrepreneur, your promotion comes in the form of happy customers singing your praises.

People *pay* for your WHAT, but they *stay* for your WAY. When you give more in value than you take in pay, your customer service becomes an incredible door opener for future business.

A good example of this is the clothing retailer Zappos. When you order from them, they have an internal protocol for next-day delivery if at all possible, even though you may have selected standard shipping.

They advertise free shipping, not *next-day* free shipping. You expect your shoes to arrive in a few days, but when it shows up at your doorstep the day after you ordered, you experience emotions that wouldn't be the same if all they had done was simply meet your expectation. Their over-the-top service makes you feel something for them. It opens your heart to not only purchase from them again but to tell others about it.

So what does this look like practically? How can you

incorporate this second-mile mindset into your business so that purchasers become promoters? We developed a six-step customer experience plan that will guide you through the process.

SIX-STEP CUSTOMER EXPERIENCE PLAN

<u>Step One:</u> *Congratulate.*

The minute your customers make a purchase, compliments are in order. A simple, "Thank you for your order," sounds elementary, but brain science shows it's a powerful tool to create loyalty. Research shows that gratitude releases oxytocin in the brain. Oxytocin is the "bonding" or "commitment" chemical. Its primary role is to increase trust, decrease fear, and strengthen relational bonds.[60]

When you feel thankful for someone, you are drawn to that person. And when you express that thankfulness, the same chemicals are released in their brain—it draws that person to you. Using gratitude as part of your customer experience strengthens your relationship with your customer and puts you on the path to winning their loyalty.

<u>Step Two:</u> *Validate.*

Follow up your congratulations with a simple statement such as, "You've made the right choice." You want to encourage them that their decision to buy was the right one.

Why? Because the minute they buy is the lowest point in their customer experience. They've spent the money, but they don't have anything to show for it yet. (Or if they received it immediately, they most likely haven't used it yet.) So, you want to remind them that their decision was a good one.

---

[60] Dr. Caroline Leaf, *Switch on Your Brain: The Key to Peak Happiness, Thinking, and Health* (Baker Books, 2013).

The moment of purchase is often when buyer's remorse kicks in. *Should I have bought that? Maybe I should've bought the other one. Is this company legit?*

These thoughts need to be answered immediately, and the validation component of your customer experience plan helps transition this natural human tendency from regretting the purchase to feeling excited about it.

Remember our discussion on how to handle objections in the sales process? You can apply the same *feel-felt-found* methodology during the validation step, to address their internal objections. The best way to do that is through customer testimonies. Sending a brief testimonial from a past customer inside your congratulation email goes a long way at this point.

After you've congratulated your customer and validated them for their purchase, it's time to move on to the next step and get started with value delivery.

Step Three: *Activate.*

Don't just deliver what you promised ... master the art of OVER-DELIVERY.

This step is where you have the opportunity to not only deliver what you promised, but to catch them off guard with something a little extra. It doesn't have to be crazy or complicated. But that little extra something is often enough to get them singing your praises.

Maybe you could do what Zappos does and try to deliver your product early. Or you can finish the job a few days before the due date. Or you can do like the Krispy Kreme guy did for us the other night when he threw in an extra donut for a "baker's dozen" (that "Hot Now" light was too alluring to pass up).

One of the best ways to over-deliver is to add a personal touch to your delivery process. In an age of automation, it's easy to let your technology run on autopilot. But deep relationships are not forged on tech platforms; they're built through real interaction. Going that second mile through human interaction makes a deposit in your relationship with the customer.

Much in the way that you deposit money into a bank account to keep your business afloat, you can make deposits in the hearts of your customers that keep them coming back. By adding a little personalization to your value-delivery process, you touch people emotionally. And as we discussed earlier, emotion is an impulse that moves people to action.

Crashlytics CEO Wayne Chang makes a regular practice of sending fresh cookies or pizza deliveries to clients as a way of maintaining that human touch. Each delivery includes a handwritten note from Chang to show his appreciation.[61]

The beauty of over-delivery is that if something goes wrong, the customer will be much more understanding. Why? Because they have a genuine relationship with you. By overdelivering, you moved them from thinking about you *transactionally* to thinking about you *relationally*. And that is a beautiful thing.

Step Four flows naturally from step three: *Communicate.*

I (Jason) counsel married couples alongside my wife, Tori. We actually wrote a book on marriage, focusing on "a leader's love life." Being an ambitious entrepreneur AND a loving spouse is quite the balancing act, but it's possible if you have the right tools in place.[62]

---

[61] Sam Saltis, "#AgencyGrowth: Mastering the Art of Overdelivery," Coredna, May 2, 2019, https://www.coredna.com/blogs/agency-overdelivery

[62] You can learn more about our soon-to-be-released marriage book at JasonAndTori.com.

Do you know what we've found to be the #1 problem for couples we counsel? *Communication.* We like to say that trust is the heartbeat of a relationship, but communication is the lifeblood. Without good communication, the relationship dies.

As a business owner, you are in the relationship business. Communicating with your customers and clients must be paramount. George Bernard Shaw once said, "The single biggest problem in communication is the illusion that it has taken place."[63]

If you've ever built or remodeled a house, you know how frustrating it is to hire a contractor who refuses to communicate. It's enough to make you want to jump off a bridge ... or hire a hitman. You walk into your kitchen and see paint brushes and buckets everywhere but no workers. And it's been that way for three days! All you want is to know what's going on.

When it comes to value delivery, you have to communicate consistently and clearly in order to build trust with your customer. Without communication, negativity fills the void.[64]

The goal of all good communication is *connection.* And the best way to connect with your customer is to answer the question *before* they ask. People are usually paying you to think for them, or to help them solve a problem, and you build trust by clearly communicating throughout the customer experience.

We failed big in this area when we first launched *Expert Ownership Live.* Our post-sale communication didn't have clear enough instructions on what to do, and it frustrated the non-techypeople. We ended up giving several refunds because

---

[63] BrainyQuote.com
[64] Bestselling author and leadership guru Jon Gordon said this on our Expert Ownership podcast (JonGordon.com).

of it. That was the price we paid for being too hands-off with the implementation of our email campaign. (We learned how *not* to make that mistake again.)

Of course, simply communicating—and even over-communicating—doesn't ensure everything is going to work out perfectly in your business. But it *does* provide an excellent experience for your customers and it builds trust at the same time. It's true in both marriage and business; relationships move at the speed of trust.

Step Five: *Escalate.*

Oftentimes, when we think of escalation, it's because something went wrong. But we're not talking about *conflict* escalation; we're talking about *customer* escalation. This is where you move your customer up your value ladder.

If you've *congratulated* your customer by expressing your gratitude for their purchase; if you've *validated* them, ensuring they made the right decision; if you've *activated* and delivered exactly what you promised (and surpassed their expectations); all while *communicating* with them every step of the way ... then rest assured you can *escalate* them up your value ladder.

Escalation is a simple matter of letting them know what else you have to offer. It's the dentist's email campaign that says, "Are you happy with the cleaning you received? We offer tooth whitening as well. But who wants white teeth if they're crooked teeth? We can straighten them out too!"

In the escalation phase, you aren't "selling" anything. You're simply making them aware of the other ways you can meet their needs or solve their problems. If you've over-delivered, then they'll want to know what else you can do for them.

Which brings us to our last step ...

Step Six: *Advocate.*

The first five steps are what *you* as the business owner do for your customer. Step Six is what the *customer* does for you. It's their positive response to your high-level value delivery.

When you congratulate, validate, activate, communicate, and escalate well—chances are, they'll advocate for you. This is when they unofficially join your marketing team. They want others to experience the joy they've experienced, which is a human tendency we all have. We want those we know and love to enjoy things together with us.

At this phase, here are a few simple ways to help them become advocates:

- Send a survey.
- Request an online review.
- Directly ask for a referral.

The key is to be willing to ask.

People are generally happy to do at least one of these *if* you've delivered them an excellent customer experience. And if you've exceeded their expectation at every level, chances are they won't need encouragement from you to do it; they'll advocate for you on their own.

That's the end goal of the value-delivery phase: to move purchasers to promoters by exceeding their expectations as you deliver more in value than you take in pay. Using the six-step customer experience is the guide to help you do it.

SYSTEMS

SeeYaPreneur

↗ 12. Money

/ 11. Leadership

/ 10. Team Building

/ 09. Systems

/ 08. Value Delivery

/ 07. Sales

/ 06. Marketing

/ 05. Value Creation

/ 04. Branding

/ 03. Ideation

/ 02. Core Four

/ 01. Identity

CHAPTER EIGHTEEN

SYSTEMS:
DEVELOP YOUR SYSTEM

Before we jump into the next section of Expert Ownership—Momentum—let's do a quick review.

Steps One-Four provided the foundation you need to build something special.

1. You know *who* you are and *what* you offer.

2. You've established your Core Four, which will guide you along the way.

3. You've unlocked your imagination and the ideas are flowing. You also know your sweet spot and can use your uniqueness to solve problems and meet needs.

4. And you understand how to leverage the power of your brand.

Steps Five-Eight took all that and put it into motion:

5. Defining your value proposition and the plan to make it happen.

6. Learning how to generate prospects through rock-star marketing.

7. Converting those prospects into purchasers by selling with style.

8. Turning those purchasers into promoters by giving them more than expected.

Now, in steps Nine-Twelve, it's time to pick up *momentum*!

This is the stage where you learn to scale your business to a point where you can remove yourself from the day-to-day operations. These steps will position you so that you can work ON your business and not be trapped IN it. Ultimately, they'll help you reach SeeYaPreneur status … where you no longer *need* a business at all.

In the next four chapters, we're going to discuss the four pillars of a scalable business:

- Systems
- Team building
- Leadership
- Money

They're so important that when we first released our Expert Ownership online course, we focused solely on these four key components.[65] Without a fully developed system, a motivated team with a common vision, strong leadership in place, and a clear money map to guide your profits, SeeYaPreneur status is not possible. But when you lock in the plan we're about to give you, you'll find yourself well on the way!

And it all starts with SYSTEMS.

When we first started our entrepreneurial journey, a buddy of ours told us there were four stages of business—concept, launch, prove, scale—and that the fourth stage is where most businesses fail. Twenty years later, with a few successes and several failures under our belts, we couldn't agree more.

It's easy to come up with an idea, launch it into a market, and prove that it works. But to scale it to a point where your idea

---

[65] Visit ExpertOwnership.com.

turns into a full-fledged company that runs without you—
that's the stuff of genius. Actually, it doesn't take a genius at
all. It just takes a simple understanding of systems and an even
simpler method of building them.

Systems aren't just important for your business; they're vital
for your sanity. Without systems, you're never fully off work—
sitting at dinner with your family, watching your kids' ball
games, sitting on the beach during family vacation—your
business always needs you. There's always some problem only
you can solve, some customer or employee with a need only
you can fill.

A lack of systems causes stress on your life, on your
relationships, and on your health.

We've seen too many entrepreneurs whose path to "success"
includes broken marriages, missed ball games, fractured
friendships, and failing health. What's worse, we've heard all
these consequences described as natural and inevitable if you
want to grow a business and increase your net worth.

But that's a bunch of BULL. We know it may be the story for
manyself-made self-starters. It may even be your story.

But it doesn't have to be.

Honestly, when we were operating a hundred offices and
closing more than six hundred deals a month, it was less
work and stress for us than when we were self-employed
and struggling to close six deals per month. How was this
possible? We had learned to utilize the power of *systems*.

If you want to own your business without it owning you, then
you must build systems that enable others to do what you do.
If you don't think that's possible, keep reading. If you do, well
… keep reading anyway! What we're going to share with you
in this chapter will help you no matter where you are on the
systems grid.

Maybe you don't have a system at all; everything is locked in your head. If that's the case, we'll teach you how to create one.

Or maybe *people* are your system and now you can't operate without certain irreplaceable employees. We'll show you how to utilize those people to create your system so when/if they quit, you won't miss a beat.

Or maybe you already have a system but it's too complex, so your people are getting bogged down with too many details. If that's the case, we'll walk you through a step-by-step process to help you simplify it.

Or maybe you have a good system, but it just needs to be developed further.

In short, wherever you are ... we're here to help you. We've created an easy method of building a simple, functional system that will allow you to scale your business to a point where you can find the kind of freedom we found. We used this very method to get us from Wannapreneurs to SeeYaPreneurs in just six years.

In this chapter, we're going to show you how we did it. We'll give you the two keys we used to unlock the power of systems so we could scale our business *and* thrive in life ... at the *same time.*

It *can* be done! Don't believe the lie that says you have to sacrifice your health and relationships to build a successful company. You can create a productive and thriving business without it costing your personal life.

Let's start with a simple definition.

SYSTEMS DEFINED

A system is a series of steps that give you consistent results and allow you to solve a problem, not just once, but over and over again—even without you there.[66] The technical definition is "a set of principles or procedures according to which something is done; an organized framework or method."[67]

Your system is the *way* you do business. It consists of all the processes that enable you to deliver your product or service. Simply put, it's the organized list of tasks needed to do the job.

All businesses are made up of systems. The problem is that many entrepreneurs keep their systems locked in their heads. They may have written a few things down here and there, but they've never taken the time to organize and manualize their processes strategically so that others could do it without them there. As a result, they can't scale their business to the next level.

But we're going to show you how to think through your list of tasks strategically and organize them systematically into a document that will become the *blueprint* for running your business. When you document your system like this, it gives you the ability to replace yourself and your own effort with other people—even less experienced people—while achieving the same, predictable results.

A successful business is *systems*-dependent, not *people*-dependent.

A lot of solopreneurs never find a way to replace themselves.

---

[66] We've combined several definitions of systems here, including concepts taken from the books *The E-Myth* and *Traction*, as well as various other definitions.

[67] Dictionary.com

And even those who do too often do it by finding someone else like them—who also can't be replaced. The result is the same in both cases: their growth is capped. They can't scale effectively because their business requires those specific, irreplaceable people in order to operate.

But if you leverage the power of systems, this won't be true for you. The ultimate liberation for a business owner is when your systems run the business, while your people run the systems. Those systems become like the walking escalators at the airport—all your people have to do is hop on and they'll get where they need to go.

This is why we teach systems before team building and leadership. You want a system to plug people into before you hire them; otherwise, you'll frustrate your best producers. People don't thrive in chaos. Even God brought order to creation before He brought mankind into the picture; He knew human beings couldn't function apart from organization!

Of course, we're not saying you can't hire someone until you have a robust system fully in place. We're just saying that you need to create a system that's simple enough to guide people through your business process. They need to know exactly what they are supposed to do. Your robust system will grow out of that (and the people you hire can even help you build it).

When we talk about a "system," we're referring to your overall business system as well as all the smaller systems that comprise the bigger one. We'll show you how it works below, but just know that the word *system* and *systems* are interchangeable in the way we use the term (i.e.: our marketing department had more than a dozen little systems that fit into our overall business system for our first business).

Developing a system is your first STEP toward truly owning your business. Systems give you:

- Scale—you get multiplied results without multiplied work.
- Time—you have more freedom.
- Efficiency—you can deliver in less time, with less effort and expense.
- Predictability—you get the same result over and over again.

Practically speaking, building a system is the most important thing you can do in business. That is, if you value your time more than anything in the world. Systems allow your business to run smoothly and to solve your customer's problem not just once, but forever.

You've probably heard the name Ray Kroc, famously known as the genius behind the McDonald's franchise. But did you know that Kroc didn't have anything to do with *making* hamburgers? He's simply the guy who organized the *business of burgers* in such a way that they were able to crank out thousands and even millions of those little meat patties with the same amount of effort as the McDonald's brothers did to make dozens. As a result, they expanded their little operation from one location in San Bernardino, California, to thousands of locations worldwide.

How was he able to do it? By developing and implementing systems.

Kroc's brilliant use of systems gave the McDonald brothers scale, time, efficiency, and predictability. That's why today you can go to a Mickey D's in Chicago, Los Angeles, Manila, or Paris and get the same predictable results. (Well, maybe not Manila—we're still not sure what we ate that day! Many of the overseas locations sell local fare, but the system is the same.)

Here's a little statistic for you, courtesy of *The E-MythRevisited* by Michael Gerber: More than 80 percent of small businesses fail, but 75 percent of franchisees succeed.[68]

Why would a *business* fail but a *franchise* succeed?

Systems.

With a franchise, you get a *business in a box.* The franchisee buys a fully systematized business with steps A-Z on how to run the business, which gives him a much better chance at success than if he were to go it alone.

Before starting a franchise, the franchisor must analyze every single component of the business and ask, *How would I get this done if I wasn't here?* He has to do that BECAUSE HE'S NOT GOING TO BE THERE ... the franchisee is going to be there.

The franchisor isn't just replacing himself; he's replacing every aspect of the business—every employee, every product, and even the physical location of the business.

We built our first company on a franchise model. So, out of necessity, we learned all the ins and outs of franchising and the absolute necessity of developing systems. In the process, we discovered that the path we took to open new locations and set our franchisees up for success was an incredible blueprint for others to build their businesses, even if their goal was not franchising.

In fact, the process of franchising is what taught us the two keys we mentioned earlier that allowed us to scale to multiple locations across the country. If you want to utilize the power of systems in your business, you need these two keys:

---

[68] Michael Gerber, *The E-Myth Revisited.*

- A systems *mindset*
- A systems *method*

Your mindset is the way you *think* about your business process. Your method is the way you *document* that process. And yes, before this chapter is over, we'll show you a model to help you with this so you can create a system of your own (or sharpen the one you already have).

MIND OVER METHOD

Let's start with mindset. You need to "think" systems before you "build" systems.

Franchising our first company taught us to "think" in terms of creating checklists so that it could run without us there. These checklists made it easy for others to follow the steps and get the exact same results. When we manualized those checklists, they became the blueprint for others to run our *same* business successfully.

So, when we talk about a systems mindset, we're talking about *thinking* like a franchisor—even if you have no intention of franchising.[69] Thinking like you're going to replicate your business will help you process every detail and document it meticulously. In the end, you'll have a guide for others to handle the day-to-day operation of your business. Even if you don't open another location, you'll have a full-fledged system that keeps your employees moving in the right direction when you're not there.

We learned to think like this by jumping feet-first into the deep end. On that phone call with Bill Spooner—when he told us how impressed he was with our service—we said, "If you send us every house in your inventory, we'll deliver the

---

[69] Michael Gerber, in *The E-Myth Revisited*, first shared this concept.

exact same level of service, every time, no matter what."

We thought he might send three or four more properties. He gave us nineteen. Our mouths had just written a big check, so to speak, and we learned quickly that the development of systems was the only thing that would ensure that sucker cleared.

Of course, we had no systems when we first started. We had to do everything ourselves. The whole *work-life* balance thing wasn't even on the radar at that point. We worked dark to dark just to survive. At that point, the *blessing* of business quickly became a *burden*.

This is when we learned to *think* in terms of systems. We knew the only way we could build this business *and* have a life was to systematize it so we could hire others to help us. We racked our brains on how to set things up so others could do what we were doing … and we could go home at a decent hour.

I (Jason) specifically remember my wife, Tori, telling me that if I could just get home at 4 p.m. every day, it would change her life forever. At the time, we had three kids under the age of four. My extended working hours put so much pressure on her that it was affecting our relationship. Her request gave me the spark I needed to create a system … and fast.

Because we had no idea how to start, we kept it simple. We bought a cheap computer, downloaded Excel and Word, and went to work.

We started with a simple Word doc for each property that listed all the client requirements and actions we had to take for the house, along with a section for notes. Then we created an Excel spreadsheet with a list of those properties and our clients. By some act of God, we learned to time-stamp our notes and to hyperlink the property address on the spreadsheet so it would open up the specific doc for the property.

We housed it all on a Dell computer-turned-server so we could access it from anywhere. This was back in 2003 when faxing documents was still a thing (give us a break here)! As two non-techy dudes, these were big-time moves for us.

With this extremely simple system in place, we knew exactly where we needed to focus our efforts on each property at all times at the click of a button. We replaced our inefficient brains with the efficiency of the computer, and suddenly nineteen properties seemed doable. In fact, twenty seemed doable. So we asked for more.

We grew to over 250 properties using that simple, basic system. It eventually became the framework for the robust online system we developed later when we franchised our company.

In the years since, we've found that many people have never built a system for their business because they thought creating one would be too difficult or overcomplicated. When we think back to that first system, we laugh. It was so simple!

Dr. John Gall, the author of *Systemantics: How Systems Work and Especially How They Fail*, makes this observation: "A complex system that works is invariably found to have evolved from a simple system that worked. A complex system designed from scratch never works and cannot be patched up to make it work. You have to start over with a working simple system."[70]

This idea is called Gall's Law in business. Even though we had never even heard of it, keeping things simple was the only way we were able to survive.

The process of developing our system was the beginning of

---

[70] Dr. John Gall, *Systemantics: How Systems Work and Especially How They Fail* (Quadrangle, 1977).

a way of thinking that became our guide as we grew into a nationwide brand. We learned to be *systems-thinkers* where everything could be made into a checklist for others to accomplish.

We also taught our franchisees to think this way. When they'd fly in for training, one of the first things we taught them were the three phases of business:

- Brain & Body—your business needs all of your brain and all of your body.
- Brain, No Body—your business needs your brain, but you don't have to be there.
- No Brain, No Body—your business can run without your brain or your body!

Our goal was to get them thinking about how to get to Level Three. That's the path of the Expert Owner. You cannot scale your business to run without you if your brain and body (or anyone else's) are irreplaceable. You can only scale your business like this if your *systems* are irreplaceable.

This is why, when our business was at its peak with hundreds of agents selling all across the country, we were doing less work than when we were trying to manage those first three properties. Our systems made it possible for other people to do the work just as well as or better than we could.

Now that you've got the right *mindset*, let's talk about your *method*. We're going to show you practically how we developed our system and the model you can use to develop your own. This proven model has helped business owners all over the world. We cover it extensively in our digital course, while workshopping a business owner on camera.

THE 4S MODEL

The method we created is called the *4S Model*. It isn't a
system in itself; it's a model to help you create your system (or
systems). You can use this model to create as many systems as
you want within your business.

The mindset of *thinking like a franchisor* is the foundation
for our model as it gets you thinking in terms of checklists.
Our 4S Model comes into play *before* you start making your
checklists. It's a strategic way to help you think through the
creation of your systems.

Here are the four parts:

- Silos
- Segments
- Stacks
- Steps

The power of the 4S Model is found in the fourth component:
Steps. Steps are the specific tasks that make up your
checklists. The Silos, Segments, and Stacks are simply a way of
organizing the flow of information so you can strategically list
these Steps.

Here's how it works: You start by breaking down the major
facets of your business into Silos (like the ones you see
on farms that hold corn, wheat, etc.). These are the major
departments of your business.

List out your Silos—three, four, eight, ten, whatever the big
components are—and label them. We've found that most
businesses have five to seven major departments (or processes).
These typically comprise of HR, marketing, sales, operations,
accounting, customer retention (or experience).

You then break each Silo into Segments. These are the smaller components inside each Silo. Label each segment with the appropriate name.

Those Segments are further divided into Stacks. Stacks are what contain and organize your Steps. You'll label your stacks as well.

Lastly, list all your Steps inside each Stack. Your Steps are the grassroots, feet-to-the-pavement tasks needed to deliver your product or service.

Here's a picture of how it looks:

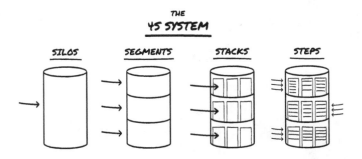

Here's an example of how we did it for our real estate business when we started:

We broke our company into four Silos:

- Pre-Marketing
- Marketing
- Offers & Contracts
- Accounting

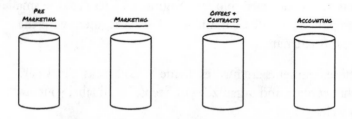

Each of those Silos consisted of several Segments. For instance, our Pre-Marketing Silo had four Segments:

- Occupancy Check
- Vacant Property
- Repairs
- Valuations

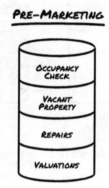

Those four Segments were further broken down into a series of Stacks. Our Repairs Segment had three Stacks:

- Preservation
- Maintenance
- Rehab

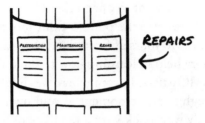

From here, we simply filled out each Stack with a series of Steps. These were the specific tasks that made up our checklists for every business process. There's no limit to the number of Steps you can have. Some of our Stacks contained five Steps, while others had twenty.

As we grew, the list of Steps grew, and so did the number of Stacks. In time, certain Steps became Stacks of their own, and Stacks became Segments. We even had a few Segments become Silos. That's the beauty of the 4S Model—it's dynamic so it can grow as your business grows.

> Note: If you have a new business you might not need to get too granular, so you can remove Stacks and just list your Steps within your Segment. As you grow and the Steps increase you can break them into Stacks.

Ultimately, your list of Silos, Segments, Stacks, and Steps becomes the *blueprint* for running your business. It's what you can plug your people into, enabling them to stay on track to deliver the same predictable results even while you're not there. And it's simple, exactly as Dr. Gall explained that successful systems must be.

This was the method we used to expand our business nationwide and remove ourselves from the business altogether. The 4S Model was our guide as we created all the smaller systems that comprised our overall business system— ultimately enabling us to experience the freedom of the third phase: no brain, no body.

You may or may not want to open other locations like we did, but you can still leverage the power of this tool to scale your business and remove yourself from the day-to-day operations. If you need more help in learning how to do it, take our online course at ExpertOwnership.com where we dive deeper and walk you through the development of your own system. You'll even get a handy workbook with a template of our 4S Model to print off and work through.

The business we workshop in the course is a coffee shop that utilized our model to streamline its process. Watching it will help you create your own set of Silos, Segments, Stacks, and Steps.

We know your business may be different than ours and your systems aren't the same. But how you create those systems—starting with the simple and scaling to the complex—by using our 4S Model is the best path to owning your business instead of it owning you.

And when you have a system in place, you'll discover that managing and leading your people will take on a whole new meaning.

TEAM BUILDING

SeeYaPreneur

↗ 12. Money

/ 11. Leadership

/ **10. Team Building**

/ 09. Systems

/ 08. Value Delivery

/ 07. Sales

/ 06. Marketing

/ 05. Value Creation

/ 04. Branding

/ 03. Ideation

/ 02. Core Four

/ 01. Identity

CHAPTER NINETEEN

TEAM BUILDING:
ASSEMBLE YOUR TEAM

Unless you're a one-in-a-million outlier, your business cannot grow without a team. You can have the best system known to man, but without others involved, your business remains a job, and your income stays tied to the number of hours you work. That's not the path of the Expert Owner.

Successful entrepreneurs have the unique ability to succeed *with* and *through* others. God wired us that way. All throughout the Bible, you see the importance of staying connected with people and the power that comes when you lock arms with others. "Though one may be overpowered, two can defend themselves. A cord of three strands is not quickly broken" (Ecclesiastes 4:12).

Jesus modeled this as He transformed the known world through a small team of twelve. You would think if anyone could go it alone, it would be the Savior of mankind. But God ordered things in such a way that even His own Son built a team around Himself to accomplish His mission.

Here's the truth: You can go *faster* alone, but *further* together.[71] Your goal in developing your business is not speed, but length and strength. You want your company to be *built to last*, as business guru Jim Collins says.[72] And the only way to do this is by empowering others and building a team.

---

[71] This is an old African proverb.
[72] Jim Collins, *Built to Last: Successful Habits of Visionary Companies* (Harper Business, 1994).

There will be times when you're tempted to take control and fix things yourself. But if you want to be a SeeYaPreneur, you've got to trust your system and lean on your team. It's impossible to move from *doer* to *developer* to *dreamer* (remember from our chapter on identity?) apart from building a team.

Our high school basketball coach used to tell us, "Together Everyone Accomplishes More." That's what TEAM is all about—helping you accomplish more with others than you could on your own.

The power of teamwork is found in one word—*synergy*. Synergy is "the interaction of elements that when combined produce a total effect that is greater than the sum of the individual elements."[73] Synergy is all about exponential growth and impact, and the only way to harness its power is by leveraging the strengths of others.

In our first book, *Whatever the Cost*, we wrote about the horse-pull competition at the Calgary Stampede, where the winning horse pulled eight thousand pounds while the horse that placed second pulled seven thousand pounds. After the event, the owners got together to see how much those horses could pull together. If you do the math, you'll probably figure they could pull fifteen thousand pounds as a team. But to everyone's amazement, they pulled an impressive thirty thousand pounds!

That's synergy—exponential impact through collaboration. Working together allowed those two horses to accomplish much more than they ever could on their own. That's what we're going to talk about in this chapter as we walk you through some of the most valuable things we've learned about building a team.

---

[73] Dictionary.com

We'll answer these five questions:

- When should you hire?
- Who should you hire?
- Where should you put them?
- What type of teams should you create?
- Who should you fire?

Some of these questions are easier to answer than others ... but they're all important to cover when building a team.

WHEN SHOULD YOU HIRE?

We hired our first employee before we actually *needed* him. We could've accomplished all our tasks each day without the help of anyone else, but it would have required us to work long hours. From a financial perspective, we enjoyed keeping all the profit for ourselves. But from a relational perspective, it wasn't the path we wanted to take.

So we had a conversation early on about what we valued most—standard of living or quality of life. Standard of living's most important component is *money*. Quality of life's most important component is *time*. For us, and probably for you, we knew right away that time was more important than money. Seeing our kids only for an hour before bedtime made that an easy decision.

From that point forward, we knew it was time to hire a new employee whenever our time with family began giving way to our business. And, as we said in the last chapter, we put a specific time in place for that—4 p.m. Whenever we got to the point where we had to work later than 4 p.m., we knew we needed to hire another person to help us maintain our predetermined quality of life.

Of course, we put in some early mornings back in those days, showing up at the office in the wee hours of the morning to make sure we hit our target departure time. But even then, if we found ourselves nodding off to sleep at 8 p.m. because we had gotten up too early, we knew it was a signal that we needed to hire someone else.

We also had a three-question grid we asked ourselves before we hired:

By *hiring this person, will they* ...

- Save me money?
- Make me money?
- Give me time?

If one or more of these questions were answered "yes," it was time to hire. The question then became, who should we hire?

WHO SHOULD YOU HIRE?

When we built our first company, we quickly learned that hiring the right *type* of person was far more important than experience or skill. Skills can be learned. Experience happens with time. But personality, work ethic, and the ability to get along with others is far more difficult to teach.

Personality tests are key in hiring, and we encourage all entrepreneurs to utilize them in the hiring process. Our personal faves are two we mentioned in a previous chapter—StrengthsFinder (now called the CliftonStrengths Assessment) and the Enneagram. While diving into the intricacies of personality tests is beyond the scope of this book, having your applicants take tests like these can save you from hiring the type of people who make you want to check into an asylum.

So, what type of person should you hire? First, let's look at the four types of workers:

- Type One—They do what needs to be done without needing to be asked.
- Type Two—They askwhat needs to be done; then they do it.
- Type Three—You have to askthem first; then they'll do it.
- Type Four—They never want to be asked to do anything![74]

You'd naturally think you want to hire all type-one workers, but we found that you can also accomplish a lot with twos and threes; you just have to put them in the right seat on the bus.[75]

Type-one workers are your all-stars, but they're rare. And oftentimes, they're the type of person who wants to own a business of their own. So be careful in hiring someone like that unless you have a plan to bring them into some type of ownership. Otherwise, you might just be training your future competition.

One challenge in hiring the right "type" is that it's impossible to know the exact type of people they are until after you've worked with them. But there are a few things you can do to help you make a more informed choice when deciding if you want to welcome them into the team.

Call their references and share these four types, asking which one fits the applicant. When interviewing, ask about their past *projects* rather than their past *positions*. Ones and twos thrive

---

[74] Special thanks to our good buddy and fellow entrepreneur Mike Andrews for sharing these categories with us.

[75] Jim Collins, in *Good to Great,* first came up with the bus analogy for team building in business.

on what they've accomplished, but threes and fours are only concerned with landing a position.

Or (and this is a fun one), you can leave a piece of trash (like a wrapper or something that's not gross) outside your door before an interview and see if the person you're thinking of hiring picks it up on their way in. Threes and fours will walk right past it every time! (This isn't foolproof, obviously, but it gives you a good gauge of what kind of person you'll be working with.)

The key is to hire *producers*, not *consumers*. You want people who are all about giving, not getting. Pay attention to their energy levels when you ask them about past projects. Producers love serving people and being a part of a team that's serving others. They'll be excited when talking about tasks they've accomplished. Consumers are low energy and just want a paycheck. They might not even keep track of past projects—just clocking in and out every day instead of working with purpose.

You also want to hire people who are emotionally intelligent. We discussed the importance of emotional intelligence as it relates to yourself in Step One, but it's just as important when it comes to building your team. Those with people smarts will outperform those who are brain smart almost every time.

A report from the Capgemini Research Institute stated that 74 percent of employers surveyed said emotional intelligence will become a "must-have" skill in the coming years.[76]

As a reminder, emotional intelligence consists of four key components—self-awareness, self-management, social awareness, and relationship management. When you find

---

[76] "Emotional Intelligence: The Essential Skillset for the Age of AI," Capgemini, https://www.capgemini.com/us-en/research/emotional-intelligence.

someone who's high in each of these and you have a position that requires a lot of interaction with others, hire them right away.

Conducting an interview over lunch is also a great way to see how emotionally intelligent someone is. Take note of the following:

- How do they treat the server?
- Are they aware of people at the nearby tables?
- Do they ask open-ended questions?
- Do they smile a lot?
- Is it a genuinely pleasant conversation?

All of these things will show you where your potential employee stands on the emotional intelligence scale.

WHERE SHOULD YOU PUT THEM?

Once you begin hiring people, you'll see the real beauty of our 4S Model, covered in the last chapter. Not only will you have a system that will guide your team through your business process, but you will also have a schematic that shows exactly *where you can plug them in.*

You'll quickly learn that having a clear system makes it easier to attract top talent. People naturally gravitate toward order, and they flourish when what is expected of them is clearly defined.

Your Silos and Segments will show them where they fit into the overall scheme of your business and to whom they report. Your Stacks will be their job description. And the Steps will outline exactly what is expected of them every day.

Back to our first hire. It was actually our college roommate, Tim. He was a religion major at Liberty University and played on our baseball team—two skills you wouldn't think prepared him for business. But he possessed the intangible skills we mentioned earlier: He was a number one worker, great with people, and diligent. But the best part about Tim was his loyalty to us. We knew if we were going to build something special, we wanted Tim to be a part of it.

Fortunately, right around the time we realized we needed someone on our team, Tim was finishing his career as a minor league pitcher with the Los Angeles Dodgers. The first job we had for him was to mow the lawns we could no longer mow ourselves. But that didn't last long. Because of our rapid growth, we pulled him into the office and put him on a Stack, where his job was simply to complete a series of Steps. He measured houses, took pictures, listed damages, and other related tasks.

And as *we* grew, *he* grew. We eventually put him over a Segment, while hiring others to handle his former Steps. He grew to lead a Silo, while others managed his Segment. Then he took over another Silo, and so on; before long, he was the leader of our entire company ... with a host of teammates managing and working the Silos, Segments, Stacks, and Steps under him.

Slowly but surely, we organized our team this way around our system:

- Leaders over Silos
- Managers over Segments
- Workforce over Stacks & Steps

You don't have to hire your college roommate (and some of you might want to do anything but!); however, you do need to use your system as a tool to build your team.

Knowing who you need to hire and where you need to put them is only half the battle. The next key question is ...

WHAT TYPE OF TEAMS SHOULD YOU CREATE?

In business, you have two different types of teams—an *internal* team and an *external* team. Depending on where you are in the lifespan of your business, you may need to lean more into one than the other.

Your external team consists of your contract labor. These are your "1099" workers—those you pay by the job; they are not on your payroll. Their income is tied to their own output, so you have much less risk in hiring them. If you have a few bad months, you're not stuck with them on your payroll, and it's not going to cost them their jobs. However, because you have no control over the work they do, your level of influence in their life and over their work is limited.

Your internal team is made up of the people you hire in-house and pay as W2 employees. An employee's income is directly tied to the output of the company, so there's more risk in hiring them. If you don't land the client or close the deal or increase your sales, you still have to pay them, and they could lose their jobs if things go south.

A lot of business leaders can't handle that kind of pressure. But if you can manage it, building an internal team of employees gives you the greatest ability to impact their personal lives in a significant way.

Most businesses start by building their external team first. This definitely makes sense. You can hire contractors to do a job immediately, with no training required. The advent of technology has made it common for many to run their business using *only* an external team. This is called the *fractured business model.* Its popularity, especially since the COVID pandemic began, has been rapidly increasing. We've had a few smaller businesses made up of only external teams, and it's worked well.

We started Benham Real Estate Group using just an external team. But as we grew, we began to hire people full-time. Every few months, we'd evaluate what we paid our external team to see if we'd save money by bringing the job in-house. During that discussion, we learned to ask a few simple questions when choosing between hiring an employee or a contractor.

- <u>Is the work essential to our business or is it a peripheral job?</u> Apple has all its computer technicians in-house because it is a technology company; technicians are essential to its business. A chiropractor operates differently. He cracks backs, not computer code, so he keeps his technology managed by an external team.

- <u>Do we need someone for a short-term project or a long-term need?</u> This one seems obvious, but some entrepreneurs make the mistake of hiring someone full-time because of a momentary need, when they could have gotten by simply hiring a contractor for the time being. If your project has an end date, look at a contractor first. If it will continue for the long term, consider hiring an employee.

- <u>Do we need a pro with specific skills we can't train?</u> And <u>do we need them fast?</u> If so, we hired a contractor. Case closed.

- <u>Will the job directly affect our brand?</u> This is a big one. You'll remember from Chapter Thirteen that branding is all about what your customer *feels* about you—and that is tied directly to their experience with your company. When it comes to building your brand, a contractor is the easiest place to start—they have skills your team won't have. But when it comes to managing and staying on brand with your value delivery, you want to control as much of your customer's experience as possible—an internal team is likely the best route to take. Their loyalty will help protect your brand.

For example, we never hired a call center to manage the calls we received on a daily basis. Because we built our brand around being relational, phone calls were a big deal for us. Rather, we hired employees and trained them to operate as portfolio managers who could build relationships with our clients over the phone.

However, if we simply sold products and needed a hotline to answer routine questions, then hiring a call center would've been our choice. Whichever one you choose, just keep in mind that *protecting your brand is the most important thing you can do.*

The most vital quality for your external team is *proficiency.*

The most vital quality for your internal team is *loyalty.*

Your external team simply needs to be good at what they do. If they can get the job done well and you only need their work from time to time, hire them as contractual work.

Your internal team needs to have full buy-in on your vision and mission. You can train them to be proficient, but if they don't jive with what you do and why you're doing it, then they cannot be on your internal team.

Last, but certainly not least, we've come to the question we all have to deal with eventually (even if we hate it) ...

WHO SHOULD YOU FIRE?

The obvious answer is that you should fire someone when they can't do the job. This is why the motto "hire slow, fire fast" is so true. If you believe you've hired the right person, but they simply cannot do the job and there's no other spot for them in your company, fire fast.

Do not give in to the temptation to keep someone on the team because you feel bad at the thought of letting them go. When you do that, you play God in their life. You are standing in the way of where He wants to take them if you don't let them move on to other things.

We dive deeper into hiring and firing in our course at ExpertOwnership.com. But for the purpose of this book, there are five types of people—other than the incompetent—who you should fire as fast as humanly possible. We derive these directly from the Bible.

You should always fire:

- Mockers—those who are pessimists, dividers, or contemptuous. Proverbs 22:10 says, "Drive out a mocker and a quarrel dies down."
- Gossips—those who are two-faced, always talking about people. Proverbs 26:20 says, "Without a gossip, conflict ceases."
- Dishonest—always fire a liar. Proverbs 16:28 says, "A dishonest man spreads strife."
- Unteachable—don't keep a know-it-all on your team. Proverbs 26:12 says, "A man who is wise in his own eyes, there is more hope for a fool than for him."
- Divider—those who constantly stir up trouble. Proverbs 6:16-19 says, "There are six things the Lord hates ... one who spreads strife among brothers."

Firing someone who exhibits one of these qualities may be the very thing that person needs to snap them into shape. Resist the temptation to hang on too long, trying to be the one who will help them change. Let their pastor or their family or their friends do that. Even if they are your friend, letting them go will be an important step in their maturation process. You'll be doing their next employer a big favor.

Later on, if you find that they have made changes in their weak area, and they want to come back, you could possibly hire them again. But that's something you can think about down the road.

So, that's the skinny on team building.

Successful entrepreneurs know how to succeed *with* and *through* others because they realize they can go faster alone ... but further together. Having the right people in the right places changes everything for your business.

When you assemble your team on these building blocks, you'll have a firm foundation as a leader.

And that's what we'll cover next as we walk you through the principles we learned that helped us motivate and lead our team ... and the *key leadership idea* that still makes us hungry every time we talk about it!

LEADERSHIP

CHAPTER TWENTY

LEADERSHIP:
LEAD YOUR PEOPLE

The beauty of building a team is that you get to lead the team you build. When it comes to living a life of impact, there's no greater privilege. When God puts you in a position to help others get where He wants them to be, consider yourself blessed.

Leadership is hard work. It's the very thing that separates an Expert Owner from the rest—they step up to the plate, toe the line, take a risk, and build to last in the midst of all the uncertainties and challenging situations that owning a business brings. Not many people are willing to do that.

You see, anybody can captain a ship on a calm sea, but it's the real leader who can keep it straight and steady in the midst of the storm. And you are that kind of leader!

But while you're out there building and growing your business, maybe you realize you aren't experiencing the freedom you set out to achieve. We've talked about how most entrepreneurs can't seem to get out from under the stress and burden of trying to grow their business and manage their team.

Many of them think their problems are with their people, and sometimes that's true. Yet as we've been discussing, it's more often the case that the trouble is with their systems—or lack thereof. But now, we're going to talk about the hardest truth of all—at least, it was the hardest truth for us to learn.

We found that when something was wrong with our business, more often than not the *real* problem was with us. We could blame it on our system or our people or some stroke of bad luck, but when we really dug deep, we knew the finger pointed in our direction.

Our business is a reflection of ourselves. When *we're* succeeding, *it's* succeeding. When *we're* growing, *it's* growing. And when *we're* healthy, our *business* is healthy.

John Maxwell, says, "Everything rises and falls on leadership."[77]

So, early in our business, when our systems weren't working well, that was on us—we had to organize, streamline, and communicate better.

If our people were failing, that was also on us—we needed to be more deliberate in our hiring, team building, and corporate culture.

Because *everything rises and falls on leadership.*

Now, the very fact that you've started (or hope to start) a business at all tells us that you have what it takes to make it as a leader. But the simple fact is, there's no way to make your business better without first making *yourself* better. So, in this chapter we're going to discuss three concepts you'll need to understand in order to become the leader God made you to be:

1. Your role as a leader.

2. The five core needs in those you lead.

3. How to motivate those you lead.

---

[77] John Maxwell, *Developing the Leader Within You* (Thomas Nelson, 2012).

YOUR ROLE AS A LEADER

We've boiled all the leadership principles we've learned down to this one simple truth:

Leadership is the ability to create an appetite in others.

Your role as a leader is to be an *appetite creator* in those who follow you. Plain and simple.

We derived this principle from the wisest (and possibly the richest) man who ever lived—King Solomon. In Proverbs 22:6 he said, "Train up a child in the way he should go, and when he is old, he will not depart from it." Although this does not seem directly related to creating an appetite, it actually is.

The Hebrew phrase for "train up" means "to touch the palate of." In ancient times, before there was baby food and running water, Hebrew mothers would take fruits or vegetables and chew them up, super fine. Then they would put a morsel on the tip of their own finger and touch the palate of their small child with the food. This would activate the child's salivary glands and begin to create an appetite in the child for that new food.[78]

This is a powerful leadership principle couched in the context of parenthood. Our dad modeled it for us every morning when we woke up as kids. We'd roll out of bed and zombie-walk into the living room before school and we'd see our dad doing one of two things—reading his Bible in our kitchen or on his knees praying in front of our couch. Seeing that example over and over, day after day, began to put an appetite in us for the same thing. Now, decades later, we find ourselves drawn to prayer and Bible study before we start our day.

---

[78] Christian minister and speaker Bill Gothard first shared this concept and our dad taught it to us.

That's the power of leadership.

You may not know it, but you're already creating appetites in those around you. The question is, what type of appetites are you creating? That's a humbling question to ask, because the answer isn't always a good one.

We heard one of our managers handling a call from a buyer's agent one day, and when she hung up the phone, she said loud enough for all to hear, "That man is an idiot." The minute she said it, we knew where she'd gotten it from—us! (gulp.) We had said the same thing several times before when buyer's agents didn't understand the ins-and-outs of selling foreclosures. So we got the team together, admitted our blunder, and explained how we could not allow negativity to define our culture. From that point forward, we saw a positive uptick in how our team handled difficult agents.

As business owners, we've found that there are two key appetites we want to create in others:

- Success at work
- Significance in life

As their leader, you not only want to *equip* your team to thrive at work but also *empower* them for greatness in life. If you can ignite hunger for these two things in your employees, contractors, vendors, customers, clients, and anyone else you come into contact with, you will have arrived as a leader.

This is the way of the Expert Owner.

The foundation that will help you become this type of leader is knowing the five core needs that make every person tick.

FIVE CORE NEEDS

We learned this from our good friend Dr. Cathy Koch: *There are five core needs that motivate every person.*[79] From the carefree kid who hasn't even considered a career to the SeeYaPreneur living the good life with his family in complete financial freedom, all people have these five basic human needs. Understanding them will help you more than anything else when it comes to creating good appetites in those who follow you.

The needs are:

- Security
- Identity
- Belonging
- Purpose
- Competence

Security answers the question, "Who can I trust?"

Identity answers the question, "Who am I?"

Belonging answers the question, "Who wants me?"

Purpose answers the question, "Why am I alive?"

Competence answers the question, "What do I do well?"

All these core needs build on each other, with the foundation being security. Until you answer the question of *security*, you will never discover your *identity*. And if you don't know who you are, then you'll never know where you *belong*, which negates your ability to know *why* you're even alive or what you were born to do ... *and do well.*

---

[79] Dr. Kathy Koch, *Five to Thrive: How to Determine if Your Core Needs Are Being Met (And What to Do When They're Not)* (Moody Publishers, 2020).

By now you know that Expert Owners are entrepreneurs who excel at relationships. This is why understanding the core needs is so important; it will help you thrive as you relate to others. The beauty of knowing the five core needs is that you can not only apply them to your work relationships, but also in your own life. For the purposes of this chapter, we're going to look at how they apply to running your business. (See the Appendix B for how they apply to you personally.)

Your business is all about relationships—with your colleagues, employees, contractors, vendors, customers, clients, and anyone else you come into contact with as you do business. And trust is the foundation of every successful relationship.

Leading your team starts with **Security**—*who can I trust?*

From an employee's perspective, the question might be: *Can I trust my boss? Will she look out for me?*

We've said this before, and we'll say it again: Relationships move at the speed of trust. It's very simple, really. If you have a low level of trust, you have a weak relationship. If you have a high level of trust, you have a strong relationship. The stronger your relationships in business, the more powerful a company you have.

Unfortunately, according to a survey published in the *Harvard Business Review*, 58 percent of people said they would trust a stranger more than their boss.[80] That's an amazing (and sad) stat.

You hire someone because you trust them; if you didn't, you wouldn't hire them. But the majority of those people you hire might not trust *you*. Maybe they've had bad experiences with

[80] David Sturt and Todd Nordstrom, "10 Shocking Workplace Stats You Need to Know," Forbes.com, March 8, 2018, https://www.forbes.com/sites/davidsturt/2018/03/08/10-shocking-workplace-stats-you-need-to-know/?sh=6bfa723f3afe.

other bosses. They don't know if your yes actually means yes. They're not sure you will do what's best for them.

So how do you overcome this problem?

Two words: **Be trustworthy!**

As the leader in your business, you have more power in the relationship than your employee does. And whenever someone lacks power, they feel insecure. If you reinforce their insecurity by not being trustworthy, even in the little things, you confirm their worst fears. This means you need to work all the harder to earn their trust and build their feelings of security.

Most leaders are dependable in the big things, but it's the little things that matter most. Let your people know *you're in it with them* and they'll reward you with their trust.

- When you make promises, keep them.
- If you say you'll be somewhere, show up.
- Take time to listen; don't always be the one talking.
- Give honest and helpful feedback.

Then there's **Identity**—*who am I?*

From an employee's perspective, the question might be: *Does my boss know who I am? Does he empower me?*

Most of our behaviors are driven by identity. In fact, we tend to think that people identify by what they *do*, when the truth is, people act in accordance with who they think they *are*.

What does this mean for you as a leader? It means you can't help people succeed if they identify themselves as a failure. Of course, not everyone who sees themselves as successful will succeed. Success is hard. But *every single person who sees themselves as a failure will fail*.

If you aren't building up your team—celebrating their wins, cheering them on, and helping them see themselves as a success—you won't get a high level of success from them.

If you're expressing constant disappointment with your team, tearing them down, and making them feel like failures, you will get a lot more failure from them.

Ask yourself this question: "As a leader, am I empowering my people in who they are, or making them feel like they need to be something they're not?"

Good leaders empower people by celebrating and leveraging their unique giftedness. Leaders *glance* at weaknesses, but *gaze* at strengths.

Next is **Belonging**—*who wants me?*

From an employee's perspective, the question might be: *Does my boss accept me? Does he want me on the team?*

People need to feel a sense of acceptance, like they are a part of something greater than themselves. This is why the two of us love business so much. Being a part of a company gives people another avenue to meet their need for belonging.

We'll talk more about culture later in this chapter, but have you noticed how many college and professional sports teams now have shirts that say #FAMILY? Coaches know the way to get the most out of their players is to make them feel like the people on their team are their brothers or sisters. This gets them away from a selfish mindset and into a self-sacrificing mentality because they are fighting for something bigger than themselves.

This is also why knowing your Core Four—your vision, mission, values, and principles—and clearly communicating them to your team are vitally important. It sets the stage for your people to know they belong to a company that's doing great things.

So find opportunities to let your people know how important they are to your business and that you like having them around. It will go a long way in meeting their need for belonging as well as garnering their loyalty. Something as simple as inviting their opinions before a big decision is made or asking for their advice on further developing your system are great ways to foster a sense of belonging in your team.

Next is **Purpose**—*why am I alive?*

From an employee's perspective, the question might be: *Do I know why the company exists? Does my boss know why I exist?*

It's vitally important to communicate your vision, mission, and goals for your business, but have you stopped to consider that the people who work for you have these as well? You're paying them to help you achieve *your* business goals and fulfill *your* company's mission, but they often aren't in a position to make consistent strides in fulfilling their own purpose.

As their leader, you have the responsibility to help your team members achieve *their* goals!

The best leaders are not just filled with a sense of purpose for their *own* life but also radically committed to helping other people discover theirs. They breathe life into every person they come in contact with, because they see everyone as special and unique, created by God with a purpose. They view themselves as day players in others' stories rather than others as day players in theirs.

The goal of your employee may be something as simple as meeting the needs of their family. Are you helping them do that? It may be serving their community. Are you using up all their time and energy and leaving them too empty to be useful in those areas? Find out what motivates them outside of work and help them achieve it.

One of the keys to navigating any relationship is to realize that other people are different from you and they are in different places than you are. But everyone is motivated by the same core needs. Empowering your people to achieve their purpose is one of the most rewarding things you can do as a leader.

Know your team and be an active participant in *their* purpose.

And finally, **Competence**—*what do I do well?*

From an employee's perspective, the question might be: *Am I doing what I do best? Am I in the right role?*

Every human being has unique gifts. But the challenge is, not everyone knows what those gifts are. Many people just do whatever they have to do in order to survive. They haven't had anyone invest the time and resources to help them discover and develop their real strengths.

But you can change that!

Give your people opportunities to try new things and unlock their true potential. Maybe what they discover as their strength won't necessarily coincide with what you need. That's okay. Encourage them to pursue it anyway.

If it's something that can help your business win, you'll have done something great for yourself by helping them. If it's something that helps them win outside of your business, you will have helped change a life. That's far more important than your business.

We got a chance to see how this works with a guy we hired years ago. Wes came to us desperate for a job, so we hired him to take drive-by photos of houses. He gradually worked his way up until he became our go-to guy for property profiles and preservation, which was a key position in our company.

While working in this position, he discovered a mechanical talent for picking locks, so we put him through locksmith school. A few years later, he asked if we'd give him our blessing to start his own company, to which we wholeheartedly agreed. We then hired him as a contractor to continue rekeying our properties.

To this day, Wes is providing for his family with his skill as a locksmith, and he still does work for us when we need him. It gives us a special feeling inside knowing that we had a small part to play in helping him discover his area of competence.

So many of your relationships—both in business and in life at large—will improve when you consider these five core needs.

Knowing them and addressing them on an ongoing basis for your team members will make you the appetite-creating leader you were made to be. And understanding their needs is the first step to motivating them to action.

HOW TO MOTIVATE YOUR PEOPLE

All too often, the people you hire can suffer from a little something we call the "Jan 15 syndrome." That's the point where the excitement of a New Year's resolution wears off, and you drop right back into your old routine. If your team ever gets to this point, you'll discover how difficult it is to turn that ship around.

But lasting motivation can be accomplished.

As we share in our online course, there are four factors that will help you motivate your team:

1. Compelling Direction

2. Shared Mindset

3. Strong Structure

4. Supportive Context[81]

<u>A Compelling Direction</u> is all about a VISION worth achieving. You've already defined your vision earlier ... now you just have to keep it out front for your team to see.

Define the goal line. They need to know what a win looks like. If they don't know what success is, how can they achieve it? Be like our buddy Casey at Movement Mortgage (remember him from Chapter Eleven?). Everyone in his company knows exactly what they're hoping to achieve as a business because it's plastered all over the walls!

And make sure the vision is *compelling*. It can't just be about selling more units than your competitors. It has to engage their hearts and minds. This is where the second factor comes into play.

A <u>Shared Mindset</u>. It's not enough for your team to know *what* they're doing; they have to know *why* they're doing it. They can complete their tasks day in and day out, but motivation will fade fast if they don't know why they're doing it.

Knowing WHAT gives them external synergy (teamwork); knowing WHY creates *internal* synergy (motivation). *Why* always fuels *what*.

This is where your mission comes into play. As we discussed in our chapter on the Core Four, your MISSION is the fuel for your VISION. It motivates and unites your people around

---

[81] Martine Haas & Mark Mortensen, "The Secrets of Great Teamwork," *Harvard Business Review*, June 2016, https://hbr.org/2016/06/the-secrets-of-great-teamwork.

the same purpose. And when you keep both your mission and your vision out front, you can watch the synergy take over. This is why visiting your two-page business plan at least once a month is so valuable.

Be like the third guy mixing concrete in our earlier analogy. He knew he needed to stay in front of that wheelbarrow, sweating his butt off because he was building a children's hospital that would save the lives of countless kids in his community. He knew his what and his why, and it motivated him to do his job diligently and with his whole heart.

The third key to keeping your team motivated is a <u>Strong Structure</u>. We've seen way too many small businesses close their doors because they couldn't keep good people. And those people left because the business itself was a cluster mess. People don't thrive in chaos, so having a strong structure in place gives you the foundation you need to help them thrive.

Now, a lot of your structure will come down to your systems. We've already talked about that. If you don't have good systems in place, your people will leave—it's just a matter of time.

But another important factor that contributes to establishing a strong structure is efficient time management. We're not talking about the work-life balance type of time management—we're talking about managing time *while your people are at work.*

You would not believe how many entrepreneurs we've talked to where the difference between success and failure in their company comes down to meetings; in short, how much time their team loses sitting in meetings day after day. Research supports this, identifying time wasted in meetings as one of the leading causes of inefficiencies in business. According to research, the cost of poorly organized meetings in 2019 alone cost companies nearly half a trillion dollars![82]

At the same time, meetings are vitally important. They keep your team on the same page and moving toward the same goal. So what are you supposed to do?

Well, it took us several years of pulling our hair out (and sometimes each other's) until we discovered a simple solution. We call it our 3S Meeting Solution. We streamlined our meetings with three key questions:

- What is the *situation?*
- What are the available *solutions?*
- What is your *suggestion?*

In every meeting, your team needs to address the situation, outline the available solutions, and offer their suggestions.

Stress is directly tied to the number of decisions you make on a daily basis. It's called "decision fatigue,"[83] and it's not only detrimental to your business but to your health and relationships as well. So make sure those on your team know that when they want to meet with you, they *must* have responses to these questions prepared beforehand or you won't meet.

- What's needed?
- What are our options?

---

[82] Peter Economy, "A New Study of 19 Million Meetings Reveals That Meetings Waste More Time Than Ever (but There Is a Solution),"Inc.com, January 11, 2019, https://www.inc.com/peter-economy/a-new-study-of-19000000-meetings-reveals-that-meetings-waste-more-time-than-ever-but-there-is-a-solution.html.

[83] Decision fatigue is a term first coined by social psychologist Roy F. Baumeister. It is the emotional and mental strain resulting from a burden of choices: https://www.healthline.com/health/decision-fatigue#how-it-works

- What do you recommend?

If they don't have that information, they aren't ready for a meeting. They're not looking for you to do *your* job (make the decision); they're asking you to do *their* job (think it through)! They want you to be their crutch. Don't do it.

This applies down the line as well. If you create a productive, streamlined meeting culture at the top, your team members will conduct their meetings with their direct reports the same way. Then no one is stuck wasting time doing someone else's work.

When you and your team learn to operate strategically through your system and conduct streamlined meetings, you'll discover efficiency and effectiveness are your best friends. As a result, morale and motivation will be high and you will be at peace. And *that* makes a strong structure.

The fourth factor for motivating your team is a <u>Supportive Context</u>. This is all about building culture. And the type of culture you want to build is one of *empowerment*. You want your people to know you believe in them and that by working with you, they're going to grow in strength, confidence, and self-worth.

Your goal as an Expert Owner is for the people who work for you to become better people—better parents, friends, spouses, etc. Working in your business should be something that helps them gain more control over their health, finances, relationships, and whatever else is important to them. That's what a culture of empowerment looks like.

We held several challenges with our employees over the years. Each new year, we'd present a different challenge along with a plan on how to win ($250 cash to the winner!). The two most popular were the *inches* challenge and the one for *debt reduction*. Interestingly enough, the same guy won both of them in consecutive years. We forget the exact numbers, but he shaved off something like eighteen inches in a sixty-day period (that's some serious body fat reduction!). The following year he reduced his debt by nearly $15k over twelve months.

A short while after his second victory, he walked into our office and closed the door behind him. He looked like he was about to cry. We were nervous, thinking he was ready to quit. With voice shaking, he said, "The past few years I've struggled both physically and financially. I lacked motivation and felt defeated. But when you guys put those challenges out there and you walked through them with us, it did something in me. And I just wanted to let you know how thankful I am for both of you."

Then he turned around and walked out.

Wow! We weren't expecting that. But it was one of the most impactful moments we've ever had with an employee. We had no clue the impact a little company-wide challenge would have on our people. We just wanted to have some fun and keep things exciting in the office. But it spoke volumes to them and showed that we cared about them outside of work.

When your team knows that you have their best interests at heart, and not just their ability to help your business succeed, they are much more likely to stay motivated in their job. They'll know that working for you is a part of helping them grow.

Do you want to know the single best thing you can do to create an empowerment culture in your business? Spend time alone with God every morning before work so that you'll see your people the way God sees them. When you see them properly, you'll treat them properly. Taking the time to pray, meditate, and read God's Word before work literally transforms your mind. Romans 12:1-2 gives us that promise:

"... be transformed by the renewing of your mind."

It doesn't mean you won't have disputes or disagreements, but it does assure you that in spite of those tense moments, you'll have the power to navigate through them and leave the situation better than when you entered. And that's not just for you ... it's for the other person too; they'll feel more empowered after their run-in with you than before. The Holy Spirit working through you is the only one who could change a situation like that.

If you apply these four factors into your business—a compelling direction, shared mindset, strong structure, and supportive context—you will have created a synergistic culture for your team. Couple that with a firm understanding of their five core needs and you are well on your way to becoming the appetite-creating leader you were designed to be.

STEP TWELVE

MONEY

SeeYaPreneur

↗ **12. Money**

/ 11. Leadership

/ 10. Team Building

/ 09. Systems

/ 08. Value Delivery

/ 07. Sales

/ 06. Marketing

/ 05. Value Creation

/ 04. Branding

/ 03. Ideation

/ 02. Core Four

/ 01. Identity

CHAPTER TWENTY-ONE

MONEY:
MANAGE YOUR MONEY

Did you know that Jesus talked more about money than Heaven and Hell—combined? There are more than 2,300 verses in the Bible that mention money, wealth, and possessions.

We believe one reason for this is that money represents security, and as we learned in the last chapter, security is our #1 core human need. God gave us that need so we would look to Him to meet it; this is what a life of faith and trust is all about. But as any successful entrepreneur can attest, the desire to make money—to find security and even identity in the things that money will buy—can easily creep in and take over.

This isn't a difficult leap to make. After all, the dollar is the "bottom line" in a company. The success of a business is often measured by the amount of money it makes.

To be clear, there's nothing intrinsically wrong with money. Jesus worked for pay up until He was about thirty years old. The problem comes when we find our security in the money we make rather than the One who gave us the ability to make it.

By now you know that Expert Owners view their business as God's, which includes the money their business generates. They find their security in God because He alone is their source of fulfillment. They'd rather make less money with God's presence in their business than more money without it.

Expert Owners view money as a resource to bless people rather than a commodity to collect. Their identity is not tied to the financial success of their business but firmly planted in the fact that they are God's kid running God's business managing His money. This fills them with a sense of purpose and provides them with the energy needed to generate wealth so that they can bless others.

So when we talk about money, we're talking about money *as a tool that puts you in a position to do awesome things in the world.* When you view money like this, your goal should be to make as much of it as humanly possible! (Like David Drye's goal of giving away $1 million a month.)

This is why we teach personal and corporate tithing like we do—when you give God a minimum of 10% off the top watch how He entrusts you with more. (Of course, it's a great practice to give much more than just 10%.)

Here's what we discovered: When financial success came our way, the greatest blessing was not the fact that we could give it away, but that it bought us time to give *ourselves* away.

I (Jason) am sitting in my home office right now at 7:23 a.m. on a Tuesday without a thought in the world of how I'm going to make money today. The residual income I receive each month buys me time *so I can give my time to you* by writing this book. That's not a pat on my back. It's simply an acknowledgement of where you can be if you apply the principles we'll teach you in this chapter.

We're going to show you the exact steps we took to achieve financial freedom so you can buy your time back. The type of freedom that will take you from entrepreneur to SeeYaPreneur.

But here's the key—we knew from the start what we'd do with our time if God blessed us financially. By God's grace, we're doing it now by helping you with your business. The question is, do you know what you would do?

If you follow the steps we outline here, and God chooses to bless your efforts, you *will* become financially free. No more trading time for money. So, ask yourself this question:

What will I do with my newfound time?

Hopefully, you've already written it down from our chapter on the Core Four, where we discussed your personal vision. But if you haven't, take time to think it through now.

If it involves living selfishly the rest of your life, please close this book—that's not the type of person we want to help. But if it involves being more present for your family and blessing people in the unique way God has gifted you, then keep reading, because what we're going to show you will help you get there.

Let's get down to business. For most entrepreneurs, if they could just get to the level where their systems, teams, and leadership have evolved to a place where they have joy and peace in their day-to-day lives, they'd feel as though they had arrived. As you read this book, you might be thinking to yourself, *Yes, that would be enough.* And, that is amazing.

But *please* hear us—it's just the beginning. True financial freedom doesn't mean freedom from the pressure and stress of running a poorly optimized business; it means freedom from *needing* your business to sustain you financially at all.

It means transforming from an Entrepreneur to a SeeYaPreneur.

Remember:

- The WannaPreneur is an employee. They trade their time for money in the form of a paycheck.

- The SoloPreneur has gone out on their own, but their business is their job, so they still trade time for money.

- The Entrepreneur trades other people's time for money because they've turned their business into a system.

- But the SeeYaPreneur trades money for money because they've used their active income from business to create passive income from investments ... and they keep all their time for themselves.

The SeeYaPreneur views his business as a launchpad, not a landing zone. It's not the end goal, but a tool that transfers active income (from business) to passive income (from investments) so that you no longer need your business at all; *your investments cover the bills.* That's true financial freedom.

But it doesn't mean you have to close your business; you *can* if you want because your business doesn't need to pay you anymore. However, if that business is your passion, by all means, have fun and stay involved at whatever level you desire.

We took what some might consider a unique path. At the ten-year anniversary of each franchise, we gifted the business to our franchisee—no more royalty payments, monthly fees, dues ... nothing. You should have heard the responses when we'd call them. People were blown away, asking why we would do something like that. Our response was simple: "We got into business to create enough passive income to cover our living expenses. With God's help, we made it. So, you're free to stop paying us now and start your journey to the same place!"

We can honestly say those phone calls were the highlights of our career.

If you remember from earlier when we talked about vision, we knew God created us to speak and write, but we didn't want to require payment to do those things. So we used the avenue of business to make that vision a reality. For that reason—

because of our God-given vision—it was an easy decision to walk away from the business once we hit our goal. Now we have the freedom to write a book early on a Tuesday morning without the need to go into an office for anything or anyone. That's an incredible feeling, and we thank God He helped us get here.

Maybe that's where you want to be one day. Or maybe running a business is where you know God wants you to stay. Either way, you can become a SeeYaPreneur who doesn't *need* a business if you apply the principles and follow the map we'll give you.

Here's what we're going to cover in this final step on your journey to Expert Ownership:

- Turning Your Grip into a Drip—a mindset for how to think about money.
- The Rule of Five—a concept we followed to ensure our company made it past the five-year mark.
- Three-Budget Plan—developing financial targets that serve as boundaries to stay within and goals to shoot for.
- Six-Step "Grip to Drip" Process—the money map we used to achieve SeeYaPreneur status.

In our online course, we cover these items in depth as well as several other financial principles and tools to help you in your business. For the purposes of this chapter, we'll stick to discussing these four pivotal points. If you would like to know more, jump over to ExpertOwnership.com.

GRIP TO DRIP

If you grew up in the '80s, you'll remember Bon Jovi's hit song, "You Give Love a Bad Name." You're probably humming the tune now, or at least looking it up on Apple Music. (You can thank us later.) While Bon Jovi may sing about giving love a bad name, when it comes to money, we learned that the secret to financial freedom is to give cash a *last* name.

Your cash needs to become *cash flow*.

We first heard this concept back when we read Robert Kiyosaki's book *Rich Dad, Poor Dad* while we were in pro baseball. He taught that you could turn the cash in your bank account into a passive income stream by investing that money into income-producing assets. By doing so, you turn your cash into cash flow. Or, as we've come to say, you turn your *grip* (money in the bank) into a *drip* (money from investments).

To understand this further, you need to know the difference between *riches* and *wealth*. Think of your money in terms of water. Riches are buckets of water. Wealth is a stream of water.

When you get thirsty and need a drink of water, what happens to the level of water if you dip your cup into a bucket? It goes down. You have less water every time you drink.

But what happens if, instead of dipping your cup in a bucket, you dip it into a stream? Does the water level go down? Not a chance. Because a stream is in motion, it constantly replenishes itself.[84]

Cash represents riches. It's the grip of money that you've earned by trading your time for money. It sits in a bank account, and if you use it, your level of cash decreases.

Cash *flow* represents wealth. It's a drip of money that you've earned by trading your money for money. It comes to you consistently because it's been invested in income-producing assets. If you use it, it will replenish itself.

---

[84] Robert Fraser, in *Marketplace Christianity: Discovering the Kingdom Purpose of the Marketplace* (Oasis House, 2004),first shared the concept.

Your financial goal in business is to earn riches that you can convert to wealth. Cash to cash flow. Grip to drip.

Your grip is your active income—the money you make from your job or business. What we're suggesting is that you set aside some of that active income, your grip, and use it to purchase cash-producing assets. That's your drip—things you own that produce money without your direct management or effort—passive income. If you stay at it long enough, that drip becomes a sizable stream and maybe even a massive river.

Your stream could be shares in mutual funds or index funds or other interest-producing financial products. Or you could invest in income-producing real estate and small businesses like we did. The minute we were able to step *out* of our business and get *on* it through good systems, we started buying these two things:

1. Small businesses that provided support or service to our core business

2. Real estate we could rent out

Now, for this income to truly be a part of your drip, you can't be actively running these businesses or managing your investments. If it takes your effort or direct, day-to-day management, it's part of your active income, not your passive income. We're talking about investments that *someone else operates*. You should be looking for distributions from *profit* on these investments, not income from *wages*.

There are several other good sources of drip income, but we chose long-term rental real estate because it has historically proven to be one of the most powerful engines for creating a strong stream of constantly replenishing "drip" income out there. Even Warren Buffett said, "I'd buy up a couple thousand single-family homes if it were practical to do so. Houses are better than stocks."[85]

We love to teach on the topic of real estate, and over the years we've helped countless people achieve their financial freedom in this way. We love watching people achieve drip income ... it's kind of addicting for us! We've even developed a course and coaching program to help you invest where we share our ten-step method for building wealth through real estate.[86]

But for today, the point isn't what form your stream takes—it's that you get started creating it. For that to happen, we turn to a little rule that helped us get there.

RULE OF FIVE

This rule is based on the fact that most small businesses fail in the first five years. Now, there's nothing wrong with setbacks and even failures. If you talk to most successful entrepreneurs, they'll tell you they *used to be* unsuccessful entrepreneurs. The difference between them and those who are no longer in the business of entrepreneurship is that they might have *fallen* but they did not *fail*. They either win, or they learn.

Knowing that a lot of businesses fail in the first five years got us thinking about *why* they fail. What could we learn and prepare for *from the start* that might help us beat the odds?

As we mentioned in the last chapter, we made a habit of spending time with God before going to work every day. On one of those days early on in our business, I (David) was reading a story in the Bible about the Israelites entering the

---

[85] Ali Boone, "What Would Warren Buffett Do? 12 Quotes for Smarter Investing," Bigger Pockets, https://www.biggerpockets.com/blog/warren-buffett-quotes.

[86] Visit ExpertOwnership.com for more information on our course, *Mastering Real Estate*.

Promised Land. They were about to get everything they'd ever wanted, all the things we associate with success—security, prosperity, peace.

And then God gives them a crazy command. He tells them that when they enter the land and plant fruit trees, they are not to eat any of the fruit that comes from the trees for the first four years. Then, in the fifth year, they can eat it (Leviticus 19:23-25).

Say *what?*

I was thinking about how to avoid losing our business in the first five years, and I realized there was a ton of practical wisdom in this story. If you pick the fruit off a tree too soon, it will damage its ability to produce fruit in the future. In the early life of a tree, it's really important to let its root system grow and develop. This way, it will have a firm foundation to provide life-giving nourishment in the form of fruit ... for years on end.

There's a natural inclination to eat the fruit too early, but if you do, you risk killing the tree. We saw this as a principle that applied to business.

Too many entrepreneurs who experience early success start "eating the fruit" too soon. They can't control the urge to splurge. We get it. It's a strong desire, especially if you're finally making the kind of money you dreamed of.

But we decided to honor this principle by not harvesting our financial fruit for the first four years of our business. Rather, we chose to set modest salaries for ourselves and leave the profits in the company until our roots were strong. We refused the urge to buy all sorts of nice stuff with our increased level of cash. We were determined to give our cash a last name!

During that time, we lived skinny—real skinny! We even moved our families into the same house together to consolidate our bills. We don't suggest doing that, ever. We took Dave Ramsey's advice literally: "If you live like no one else, then one day you can live like no one else."[87]

It wasn't until our fifth year that we allowed ourselves to take a few hefty distributions (those were good days!).

THREE BUDGETS

With the Rule of Five in play, the next thing we did was create financial targets. Aiming for one big number felt so demotivating, so we came up with three. We later called it our Three-Budget Plan because it turned out to be one of the best things we've ever done to help us stay on the path to financial freedom.

We created the following three budgets:

- A Livable Budget—what we'd *need*.
- A Comfortable Budget—what we'd *like*.
- An Incredible Budget—what we'd *love*.

We put a dollar value on each of these. This was our way of quantifying our goals. Many entrepreneurs fail to quantify how much is enough, so they end up endlessly pursuing money until the day they die. That's not the path of the Expert Owner.

Our *livable* budget was the monthly income we could literally survive on *if we had to*. We're talking bare-bones-type stuff. On this budget, you'd have to get rid of your lawn service crew and pool cleaning and whatever else is not 100 percent necessary.

---

[87] DaveRamsey.com

When we lived together, our livable budget was around $1,500 a month each, but we quickly changed it to $2,500. This was back in 2003, so those numbers are near impossible nowadays. But the key is to keep your livable number as lean as humanly possible.

Our *comfortable* budget was the amount of monthly income we could live on comfortably. This is the budget where we could live our lives without having to worry about pinching pennies. We could send our kids to good schools, get our lawn serviced, and afford a few containers of mocha-chocolate-chip ice cream to eat when we watched the Cowboys play.

Our *incredible* budget was the amount of monthly income we dreamed of having. An amount that would allow us to go on overseas family trips, afford college without loans, leave an inheritance for our kids, and give abundantly to nonprofit efforts that are doing great things in the world.

In our first four years of business, we hovered somewhere between our Livable and Comfortable numbers. Those were hard years. You can clearly see that our plan isn't a get-rich-quick scheme. Pure determination to become SeeYaPreneurs was often the only thing that kept us strong.

Having these budgets in place gave us goals to shoot for … as well as boundaries to stay within. This made our personal financial decisions much easier and kept us motivated to hit the targets.

With those numbers firmly ingrained in our heads, we came up with a specific plan on how we could cover each of those numbers—first with our active income from our business and then with our passive income from our investments. The process we came up with involved six steps.

SIX-STEP "GRIP TO DRIP" PROCESS

We're going to share here the actual map we followed to turn the *riches* we earned from our business into *wealth* gained by investments. If you methodically follow these steps while your business continues to make money, you will find yourself firmly established as a SeeYaPreneur for life.

Steps One-Three focus on your *active* business income.

Steps Four-Six focus on using your active business income to build your *passive* investment income.

All six steps utilize the three budget numbers derived earlier.

Step One: Cover your livable budget with active income from your business.

When we got to this point, our business was finally at a place where it could sustain us full-time without having to find outside work. (No more painting doors on the weekend.) If you're a Wannapreneur, this is the moment when you can quit your job and move into the Solopreneur category. Congrats! Most people never even get this far.

Step Two: Cover your comfortable budget with active business income.

We actually arrived a little sooner at this stage than we had planned. We landed a few big clients and, all of a sudden, date nights got much better! When we hit this stage, we moved our salaries up to a point where our brides didn't have to pinch pennies at the grocery store anymore.

Now, you would think the natural progression of steps would mean Step Three is where you cover your incredible budget with active income from your business, but that would be incorrect.

Step Three: Set aside the surplus.

This step is what separates those who achieve financial freedom from those who don't. It's tough because your business is making money *above* your comfortable salary, and that money is sitting there screaming at you, "Spend me!" But hear us on this—DO NOT TAKE IT FOR YOURSELF! It's not time to start making incredible money just yet.

This is where a little delayed gratification can go a long way. According to studies, the number one predictor of success isn't education or the wealth of your parents or even natural intelligence and talent—it's whether or not you can delay gratification.[88]

If you can't say "no" to your natural impulse to take the money, then your hopes of making it to SeeYaPreneur level will be short-lived. But if you have the discipline to leave that money alone, you'll be able to use it for crucial Step Four.

These next three steps are where you use your active income to build your passive income.

Step Four: Cover your livable budget with *passive* income from investments.

Remember, in stage one, you covered your livable budget with *active* income from your business. Now, your goal is to cover it with *passive* income from investments.

Step Four is where you take the surplus above your comfortable salary and invest it into income-producing assets outside of your business. (That is, after you've invested the necessary funds back into the business. We talk more about that in our course.)

---

[88] Walter Mischel, *The Marshmallow Test: Why Self Control Is the Engine of Success* (Little, Brown and Company, 2015).

Like we said earlier, we started by investing in two asset classes—small businesses and real estate. We started slowly, but the next thing we knew, we owned several other businesses and a handful of rental properties. Soon, our livable budget was completely covered by passive income from our investments.

Hear this: When your passive income exceeds your bare-bones living expenses, you are *financially free!* You can now live without ever having to work for money again if you don't want to.

Let that sink in.

Imagine the feeling of going to work because you WANT to and not because you HAVE to.

But we're not done yet; there are two more steps to go.

Step Five: <u>Cover your comfortable budget with passive income from investments</u>.

We need to be clear here—at this stage, we were still living off active business income for our comfortable budget in the form of salaries. Yet we now had all this passive income coming in the door on top of our business income. Instead of spending it or increasing our salaries, we simply added it to our surplus of active business income. This *accelerated* the speed of our "Grip to Drip" plan exponentially.

Before we knew it, we had enough passive income to replace our comfortable salaries. At this point, we could take ourselves off the company payroll if we wanted to, and nothing about our way of life would change. That was an amazing feeling.

This is the stage where you move from being financially free to *independently wealthy.* You can live a comfortable lifestyle for the rest of your life, *independent* of any job or day-to-day effort.

From that point forward, we began to aggressively invest in passive income vehicles with every drop of both our active business surplus *and* all the passive income earnings.

Fortunately for us, the more we systematized our business, built our team, and led our company, the more active income we found ourselves generating. So, we just dumped that additional money into buying more small businesses and real estate while keeping our salaries at the level of our comfortable budget.

Of course, we didn't suck all the money out of the business. We kept a solid six- to nine-month expense floor in our account as a net zero. But we used all the money we earned over and above that to buy more assets to increase our drip from a tiny stream to a river with an abundant flow.

But there's one more step, which just so happens to be the best one of all.

Step Six: Cover your incredible budget with passive income from your investments.

Getting to Step Six is where you can give away more money than you ever imagined and live a life you never dreamed. Even better, it's a place so incredible that you'll want nothing more than to help others experience the same.

From this point on, you only do what you *want* to do. Will you keep your business? Only if you want to. Only if God tells you to and it doesn't put stress on your family or your friends. Only if it brings you fulfillment and joy and contributes to your personal vision and mission.

Getting to Stage Six takes a loooong time. So be patient. Keep applying the principles we've taught you and trusting God to help you. All you need to do today is start moving forward.

Here is the plan in picture format:

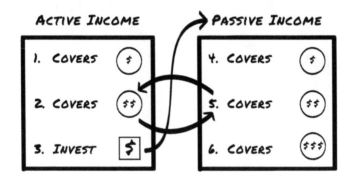

It doesn't matter if you're a wannapreneur who has yet to take the first step in business, a solopreneur who is still struggling to do it all yourself, or an established entrepreneur who just needs to get on top of your rapidly growing business …

… the concepts we've shared will help you achieve a life you never dreamed possible! One that can make an impact in the lives of others for generations to come.

It doesn't take rocket science. You don't have to be a brain surgeon. You just need a little discipline, a lot of determination, and a willingness to stick to the plan. And you, too, can turn your grip into a drip—a steady stream of money that replenishes itself without your direct involvement … every day, and night, for the rest of your life.

And best of all, when you do it God's way, you won't find your security in that money. You will own it, but it will not own you. Imagine what that life would be.

Then stop imagining it and go build it. Because that's who you are—an Expert Owner.

APPENDIX A

MISSIONEERING

In Chapter Nine we talked about how our success in business afforded us the opportunity to start several new initiatives, both in the for-profit and nonprofit space. We want to mention one initiative, in particular, that would be of interest to you as an entrepreneur.

In 2010, in the middle of the economic and housing crisis, we heard a statistic that six hundred missionary families per month were leaving the mission field because Western funding had dried up. The problem wasn't a lack of missionaries; the problem was the lack of financial sustainability to keep them on the field.

We wondered what we could do about this disparity.

Then it hit us, after much prayer, that we could do the same thing we had done time and time again in business—look in our bag to see what we had to offer. Like the young boy whose lunch Jesus used to feed the 5,000, we just offered what we had.

As entrepreneurs who created systems and rallied people toward a common vision, we could create a sustainable business to solve this problem of insufficient funding. Everything we had learned as entrepreneurs equipped us in the area of financial sustainability. *This* is what we had in our bag.

The light bulb went off in our heads. We had an idea! We could start a business overseas to meet tangible needs, hire local people, and give missionaries a place to work and minister while getting paid.

We called it *Missioneering*.

It would be a strategic attempt to bring together entrepreneurial business endeavors and Christian missionary work. Missioneering would be a combination of pioneering and engineering, with a heart for missions. It would require us to abandon the "two-sphere" mindset that there is a sacred/secular division between vocation and ministry.

God had already been teaching us about this. The more we read the Bible, the more we grew convinced that faith can (and should) be practiced in the midst of the workplace. We learned that we were ministers right where we were, in our place of work. And our business was our ministry.

Our own company had proven to be a prototype for this paradigm, and now we had the desire to replicate it overseas to accomplish the same objective.

The great need we saw was to *make mission work self-sustainable*. If we simply combined three elements, we believed that we could do it:

- Pioneering—trekking into uncharted territory
- Engineering—building infrastructure from the inside out through business
- Missions—the overall vision of missionary work for the purpose of advancing God's Kingdom on Earth

So that's what we did. And it worked!

The result was a self-sustaining revenue engine that could train and fund indigenous nationals who could reach their own culture and beyond for Christ. Our idea did not replace traditional missions, but simply strengthened it for God's glory.

Along the way, we learned that when God was doing something, it usually resonated in the hearts of other believers as well. God dropped two guys into our lives who burned with the same passion we had to help missions through business: John Sears and Jacob William.

So, when we say "we" in terms of missioneering, we're referring to the four of us. Jacob is an entrepreneur from India, and he's the only man other than our dad who can walk into our office and tell both of us to shut up and listen to him … and we obey without hesitation.

John is a serial entrepreneur who we're pretty sure was born developing and implementing strategy (even before he left the hospital)!

Our first missioneering company was created in 2010. We started it as an outsourcing business based in the Philippines. Basically, the company handles any business processes that require a phone or computer; we have a large staff of trained professionals to accomplish those tasks.

Our first objective was to bring real value to the city by *creating jobs* through a Kingdom-minded business. We've employed literally thousands of Filipinos who are truly grateful for the work. On our last trip to the Philippines, we received roaring applause from our employees because they were all so thankful for steady employment. It was humbling. As of early 2021, we have over 1,500 employees there.

Our second objective was to *disciple our employees* at work, as well as their families at home. In our first year of business, we had seventy employees come to know the Lord. Our pastoral missioneer, who is a paid member of our staff, discipled them. These numbers have grown tremendously through the years.

Our third objective was to *engage the spiritual leaders* of the city. At one point we had over 150 pastors and spiritual leaders meeting for monthly prayer, where they are encouraged and equipped by our missioneers.

Our final objective was to use our company profits to *support indigenous missionaries* to reach the unreached and unengaged.

All the profits stay in the Philippines and are re-circulated toward these objectives as well as used to start new missioneering businesses. From the fruit of that first business, we were able to start several other businesses in the area.

So how did we start?

First, we found a missionary already on the field who had the same heart to bring tangible value to his city through work. His name was Kevin Cracknell, and he had been in the Philippines for seven years. But his financial support was dwindling, along with his ability to influence the governing authorities of the city. He knew something needed to change.

We shared with him our concept—and it was the spark he was looking for. We funded the venture and then put him on our payroll with the task of finding a staff and location. He was all over it, and he knocked that task out of the park.

While he was working on all this, the four of us were back in the States drumming up business to send his way. We landed a couple contracts, taught him how to deliver the service according to the clients' requirements, and he and his team of Filipinos accomplished the work. A few months later and forty employees deep, we realized we were on to something.

Early on, we knew that only one missioneer wouldn't be enough if we wanted to grow. So God brought us two more missioneers who held strategic positions in the company. Trent Pruett served as our minister to the people (pastoral missioneer) while AjitSivarajan served as our minister to the process (process missioneer).

Our pastoral missioneer was responsible for:

- Shepherding the hearts of the people
- Organizing discipleship
- Developing community
- Helping with Human Resources

Our process missioneer was responsible for:

- Business excellence
- Quality control
- Client retention
- Customer service

Our pastoral and process missioneers worked together as engineers (business and personnel infrastructure), while our original missioneer (Kevin) acted more as a pioneer (finding and starting new businesses). Although our missioneers had different roles and responsibilities—with a lot of overlap— all of them were on mission to see God's Kingdom advance in their city. We've watched these three work together with incredible Christian unity that has yielded supernatural results.

With over 1,500 employees—many of whom have received Christ—we are also servicing dozens of clients from all over the world. And it has been inspiring to see the incredible favor we've received with the leaders of the city because of the amount of revenue and jobs we have generated.

In addition, through the profits and influence of our company, our missioneers have started a sports league, evangelism outreaches, disaster relief projects, monthly Bible studies, an orphanage, and now a budding church. Support for these programs comes from simply creating value in the marketplace.

The amazing thing is how much direct evangelism and discipleship ends up taking place when a business is owned and run by Christians who see themselves as ministers of God. Our team has an unbelievable amount of consistent contact with people on a daily basis.

It is no wonder the Apostle Paul's tent business was a mission for him! He was right where everyone else was, in the marketplace. He got paid to meet their physical needs while simultaneously meeting their spiritual needs. Having two hours of a congregation's time on a Sunday morning is good, but having forty hours of their time Monday through Friday takes discipling to a whole new level.

Just as our first missioneering business was beginning to take off, two of our missioneers found additional business opportunities in the city as well. Kevin and Trent came to us with a concept we all loved. They wanted to open fitness facilities in the busiest parts of town.

Boom! Now *that* was right up our ally.

What's great is that we were able to use the profit from our first missioneering company to fund these additional missioneering projects. We opened two CrossFit gyms in 2012. Our trainers taught gym members that "physical training is of *some* value, but Godliness has value for all things" (1 Timothy 4:8 NIV). And they got paid to teach this! Our CrossFit gyms were simply tools to bring the Gospel of God's Kingdom right into the busiest parts of the city.

As a result of the increased popularity of our gyms, our missioneers gained the respect of local media and government officials as well. Interestingly, many high-ranking officials and well-known media became members. It was fun to watch our missioneers and their wives receive invitations to holiday parties with cultural and political leaders. One of our guys was actually featured on the cover of the city's largest magazine and in the local news.

But that's not the best part. We were then able to sell those gyms and use the funds to purchase a piece of land that now houses an orphanage for abandoned kids.[89]

In the Bible, blessings are both spiritual and economic (Genesis 12:2–3). This is not a "prosperity" message, but simply a truth that Christians can lead the way by being a blessing to other people. And one of the best ways to do this is through the avenue of work. Vocation and mission don't have to be split apart in a false division. God never intended this.

Missioneering was our attempt to create something that in the long-term was both economically sustainable and beneficial to the Kingdom. We would absolutely love it if entrepreneurs around the world would read this and say, "Hey, I can do something like that. I've always seen myself only as a businessperson, but now I realize that I'm also a minister of the Gospel right where I am, and my business is a ministry to extend God's kingdom."

You don't have to go overseas to be a missioneer. A good friend of ours, JD Gibbs—son of Hall of Fame football coach Joe Gibbs—asked us to meet him for lunch one day to discuss what he could do to impact his city for the Lord. He wanted to provide money to a ministry that was close to his heart, but he wanted to do more than just give money; he wanted to create a stream of sustainability.

When we outlined the concept of missioneering to him, JD was hooked. We suggested that he take the money he wanted to donate and convert it into a wealth-generating river, which could be done by investing in a business and naming the ministry as the beneficiary. In this way, he would create a dual

---

[89] The ministry is called Safe Haven and it's run by Trent and his wife Amy.

ministry: the business itself (the employees and patrons of the business) and the funds for the other ministry.

And you know what? He did it! He opened a sandwich shop and used the funds to support that ministry.

Today, JD has gone home to be with the Lord. He was an amazing husband and father, and his legacy of stewarding God's resources (his talent and money) to expand God's Kingdom live on to this day in our hometown of Charlotte, North Carolina.

This is how Christians can live powerfully in the world. We must see ourselves as ministers of God, seamlessly weaving vocation and mission together. These were never to be separated in the first place. We have to abandon the old paradigm of the sacred/secular divide and get back to the reality that everything God has made is sacred, which includes our work.

As Kingdom entrepreneurs ...

- Our destination is *God's Kingdom*.
- Our vehicle is *God's work*.
- Our fuel is *God's love*.

There's no stopping that combo!

APPENDIX B

YOUR FIVE CORE NEEDS

As mentioned in our chapter on leadership, all people have five core human needs. They are:

- Security—*who can I trust?*
- Identity—*who am I?*
- Belonging—*who wants me?*
- Purpose—*why am I alive?*
- Competence—*what do I do well?*

*K*nowing these needs will help you become a much better leader as they will help you better understand those you lead. But what we want to talk about in this brief appendix is *how those needs apply to you personally.*

Let's start with security, as all the other needs are built upon this one.

The very fabric of your life is built upon security. You learned it from the time you were an infant; you just didn't know it. When you cried, you learned to trust that your mom would meet your needs. This is why the mother-baby bond is so tight—it's forged on the foundation of trust.

If you grew up in a healthy family, you soon learned to trust your parents to provide for you and protect you. This gave you a sense of security, and from that place of safety …

- You were able to discover who you were (identity).

- You knew you had a family who loved you no matter what (belonging).
- You understood that your life was significant and had meaning (purpose).
- You learned that you had gifts and talents that could help others (competence).

Can you see why the attack on family is so detrimental today? Hollywood, big tech, secular media, and a host of streaming services push content that redefines this most basic foundation of humanity, and it has wreaked havoc on so many people.

These days, many people are growing up with no real sense of security, which has led to a host of other needs going unmet throughout their lives. Just turn on the news and you'll see how destructive this anti-family worldview has become.

As entrepreneurs, it's easy to find our security in business or wealth or our ability to make things happen. But none of these things can quench the thirst in our souls.

And we can't place our *ultimate* security in people either. While it's important to have trusted bonds with others, we cannot find our *ultimate* security in them. Why? Because people are fallible. At some point, they will fail us. And if we've found our *ultimate* security in them, then when they fail us, our world falls apart.

Our ultimate security can only be found in the one who created us—God. This is why there are so many verses in the Bible about trusting God. He wired us to connect with Him by placing our trust in Him through His Son, Jesus Christ. When we do, everything we know and believe filters through that solid foundation.

Look at what Jesus said: "Do not let your hearts be troubled; believe in God, believe also in Me" (John 14:1). The phrase *believe in God* means to trust Him, to commit yourself to Him. Jesus is telling us that God is our ultimate security.

But it gets even better. He also said, "... believe in the Light, so that you may *become* sons of the Light" (John 12:36). Finding our security in Christ *changes who we are.* Placing our trust in Him changes our identity into one of God's kids.

This is life-changing. When we place our faith, hope, and trust in Christ, it sets the stage for all our other needs to fall into place.

It works like this:

- Security: I trust God as my Father and Jesus as my Savior.
- Identity: I am a child of God—He's my Father.
- Belonging: God wants me because I'm His kid.
- Purpose: I want to bring my Father glory in all that I do.
- Competence: I can do all things through Christ who strengthens me.

When your core needs are met through a relationship with the God who created you, it doesn't matter what your family situation was like. You can become brand-spankin' new, transformed from the inside out—just like our dad when he placed his trust in Christ months after we were born.

This is the foundation of Expert Ownership.

It's why we opened with Mark 8:36 at our franchise conference that day: "What does it profit a man if he gains the whole world but forfeits his soul?" When your core needs are met through Christ, it sets you up to help others do the same.

We're not saying your place of business needs to become an evangelistic crusade with a fish symbol on your website. We've never done that ourselves. But we *are* saying that when you, as the leader, find your ultimate security, identity, sense of belonging, purpose, and competence in God, then you have a secure footing to be exactly who God created you to be.

Others will see this and will want to know what makes you tick. And you can lead them to a place where they can have their needs met by the same God who's meeting yours.

THE OWNER'S SUITE

Join the Owner's Suite where you'll experience live, monthly coaching from the Expert Ownership team, our latest interviews, research, and exclusive extras only available here.

Explore the lineup of online courses:

- Mastering Small Business
- Mastering Marketing
- Mastering Real Estate

and many others.

For business owners considering personal coaching options to help save more time, make more money, and have greater impact, discuss custom coaching options with the Expert Ownership team.

ExpertOwnership.com

CPSIA information can be obtained
at www.ICGtesting.com
Printed in the USA
LVHW022307140821
695337LV00007B/655